untruth

Exploring Truth in a Post-Truth World

RUTH EMBERY

Untruth: Exploring truth in a post truth world

Copyright © 2021 Ruth Embery

All rights reserved. No part of this publication may be reproduced, stored in, or introduced into a retrieval system, or transmittted, in any form, or by any means (electronic, mechanical, photocopying, recording or otherwise) without the prior written permission of the publisher.

Published by: Voice in the Dark Publishing

ISBN: 978-0-6453488-0-4 (Print)

ISBN: 978-0-6453488-1-1 (Electronic)

Unless otherwise noted, all Scripture quotations are taken from THE HOLY BIBLE, NEW INTERNATIONAL VERSION® NIV®

Copyright © 1973, 1978, 1984 by International Bible Society®

Used by permission. All rights reserved worldwide.

Cover artwork © Ruth Embery

DEDICATION

This book is dedicated to seekers everywhere. May you find the One who is the answer to every question you ever had.

"...the truth will set you free..."
(John 8:32)

Contents

Foreword - Warning!	vii
Prologue	ix
Introduction	xi
In the beginning	1
What if we have it all wrong?	5
Exploring human supremacy	13
Exploring truth	19
Exploring emotions and feelings	29
Exploring my value	45
Exploring freedom	51
Exploring equality, inequality and the state of our world	57
Exploring sin and its origin	61
Exploring intellectual assent	71
Exploring righteousness and justification	83
Exploring good, evil and life	87
Exploring law and religion	93
In the end...	97
APPENDIX	105
About the author...	109

ACKNOWLEDGEMENTS

In a perhaps most unorthodox manner, I would foremost like to acknowledge the immense battle and difficulty I had writing this book. It was not a topic I willingly took on, nor the style of writing I would personally prefer. However, there was a compulsion along with constant confirmations that I was indeed to write it, so it is with great gratitude and joy that I find myself at the end of this task!

More traditionally, I must first thank my long-suffering husband, Martin, for putting up with all my moaning and continuing to encourage me, even though it was, at times, with a good measure of impatience born out of his frustration with my inability to have the same confidence as he that I actually had something of value and import to write.

And then there are the myriad of people, some nameless, others close friends, some who spoke prophetically over me and prayed for me around this book, as well as those who simply encouraged me, either by expressing their desire to read the end product or in their interest in the topic itself. This includes so many in the "Christian Authors Downunder" Facebook group. I hope you each enjoy the read and find some value within these pages.

It is with great gratitude that I also acknowledge two people I am yet to meet personally, but have come to know through the wonders of social media. Anne Hamilton (author of over 20 books), who has encouraged and inspired me with the depth of thought and understanding she brings to her posts as well as her books, and Dylan Morrison (author of a number of books including *The Prodigal Prophet*), another who continually inspires and provokes me with his posts: thank you both so much for not only taking the time to read my manuscript, but also for your beautiful, thoughtful and encouraging responses. I find it quite amusing that we have all been teachers of mathematics at some point in our lives, too!

Following these have been another four who have lent their gifts, abilities, insights and time. Anne Wills, Sondy Ward and Teri Kempe (another I have not met in person yet!), thank you so much for giving of your editing skills and time to pick out all those errors as well as *ruthlessly* point to my annoying little habits and literary quirks. Thanks also to my brother, Phillip Dixon, for treating this like one of his student's work, pushing me to dig into those areas that needed expansion and greater clarity.

Finally, but by no means least, I give acknowledgment to my Lord God, Yeshua Messiah — Jesus Christ, who is the Giver of all good gifts, and has boundless patience and love for me, even (or especially) when I needlessly flap about in insecurity. He is my Rock.

Foreword - Warning!

Perhaps this book should come with a warning, because if you are looking for answers, you may end up with more questions than you started with. But I make no apologies. As a secondary school teacher many years ago, my students would complain to me: "You're the teacher — you should give us answers, not more questions", when I responded to their questions with further questions. However, I saw my role as teaching my students to think, to use their own minds, because it was from this place that they would stretch and grow, developing skills to take them a great deal further than simply learning the correct answer either to a finite question or worse, as a way to be accepted in society.

Writing this book has been quite a battle for me. One of the questions I kept trying to nut out was what it was I was trying to say — what was the point. It wasn't until nearing the end and reading it yet again that I realised that this book is a journey not a destination: it is the journey for each individual who reads it that is important, not whether they agree with me in the end. It is not a book full of rich theology — although you may find it along the way — or neat arguments and answers for you to stand on the same side of the fence as me when you finish. The purpose of this book, is to take you, the reader, to a place of questioning things you either don't want to, or never knew you could.

I pray Ruach Ha-Kodesh — Holy Spirit — will inspire, lead and bless you as you read.

Prologue

He leaned back in his chair as he finished the final assessment of the profile his publicist had put together. It was time for it to go live, and overall, he felt it was going to be a great platform to launch him into the wide world. However, there was still that little niggle of unease. In truth, he should be pleased with the way they made language work for him: words like "multiple experiences" made the two actual occasions seem more substantial, as did the "international acclaim" from his colleague in Germany. And as for his photo, well, every great profile shot is photoshopped at least a little, and it certainly still looked just like him — even more like him in reality. None of it was actually lying and anyone who did bother to dig into the facts behind the words and pictures wouldn't really find much to pull him down. It was all about his performance from now. He hoped he could live up to the image they had created for him.

Meanwhile, his partner appraised herself in the mirror again. She had chosen the dress in the hope that the fit, the fabric and the colour would disguise, at least to some degree, the fact that she wasn't as trim as she used to be. Or would like to be. She wasn't sure that it worked, but it would have to do. There was no time left for further changes.

As she left the house, she reflected on how much time and effort she spent trying to alter her appearance. High heels to increase her scant height of five feet, make-up to enhance some features and hide others she saw as blemishes or not quite right, not to mention the hours and dollars spent on hair styling and colouring. All to make her look more…what? Attractive? Acceptable? And in the end, was she really any happier or more satisfied for it all?

No matter what culture you live in, the idea that conformity and perfection will produce belonging is a strong driver. We are born with the innate desire to belong, for others to accept us and affirm our value. How we get those needs met, though, depends on our beliefs about those needs and the answers presented to us. Some may be helpful but others can be downright destructive. Unfortunately, it is not always apparent which is which.

In Western culture, advertising and other media continually assure us of the ability of certain products and a variety of methodologies to bring about desired changes or outcomes. However, most are nothing more than clever gimmicks or ideas that, at best work for a short time, not to mention whether the proposed desires actually have merit and should be entertained.

When it comes to what really works or is necessarily to life, I would propose that we have much of it back to front and upside down. We think that what we experience is normal and right because we perceive everyone else is in the same position. This book seeks to unpack some of the *norms* of our society not only to expose and uncover some of the inconsistencies within them, but also to suggest an alternate way of seeing. Along the way, there are questions placed where you can pause and ponder your own response.

Enjoy the journey!

Introduction

I made the mistake of answering the phone today. These days, with all the scams, telemarketers and other nuisance calls, I rarely bother unless it is a number I know. But I got hooked in. It was a local number.

Immediately I wished I hadn't. Usually I simply hang up, however, not in the mood to be rude, particularly as she also had a local accent, I allowed the caller space to at least tell me what she was calling about. She dived straight in with some quite personal questions, which I evaded, followed by a few which I refused to give the scripted answer to. After about 30 seconds, as she tried harder and harder to press my buttons, I began my wind up of being polite and letting her know this wasn't a conversation I was interested in having. The caller became more and more frustrated, almost to the point of rudeness, throwing more and more rhetorical questions at me to try to hook me into the fear game she was playing. Not that she knew it was a game. I hope.

In our society, there is a growing trend of intolerance toward any form of disagreement. At one level, this has been very obvious around particular beliefs, especially regarding sexuality, abortion and climate change, not to mention a certain virus and all its associated issues. The ability to discuss, to openly debate without degenerating to abuse and nastiness seems to be a rapidly diminishing freedom. Even in my phone conversation, which was about something as lightweight as our *need* for *adequate* superannuation and issues surrounding this, the caller was quite incredulous that I was not concerned and wasn't going to buy into fear. She became so stressed by my responses that she began to make accusations and assumptions about my position even though I had given her zero information about it. She was so frustrated with my lack of concern and was so sure there was no way my future could possibly be secure that she ended up with a very sarcastic, "well, good luck with that".

The point is, we do have a choice about how we interact with our culture and the beliefs of others. The current prescribed rhetoric does not have to be the only way of thinking, knowing, or understanding. Even though there are numerous voices around us stating "truth is whatever works for you", it seems the acceptable alternative narratives have an increasingly narrow bandwidth. The cry of the 1960's was freedom from the restraints of religion and conservative viewpoints. However, in a very brief time we appear to have lost those hard won freedoms as we have ridden a full pendulum swing across to a new pressure to conform to "progressive-ism" and its narrow tenets that to all intents and purposes look very much like a new religion. Look like me, think like me or be damned!

Why do we care so much what others think and believe? Why does it matter?

In addition to all the other issues of the overreactive pendulum swing, simply changing outward actions generally doesn't fix those things that are not working in the current format. When we see a result or outworking we don't like, simply ditching the "baby with the bathwater" and moving to the complete opposite is usually just getting rid of one problem to take on another, which may actually be worse. It can be likened to the old lady who swallowed a fly, then a spider, followed by a bird, a cat, a dog, a goat, a cow and a horse. It doesn't work to do something different if we don't address the underlying flaw. It is like having a car that won't go and thinking that a new paint job will fix it. Or just like the merry-go-round of weight loss — I might keep trying different diets, but if I continue to use food to comfort, then I will inevitably self-sabotage. Unless I expose the root of the problem, it is unlikely anything will change, particularly in the long term.

Meanwhile, in the larger, global scenario, our politicians and world leaders also keep acting in ways corresponding to their underlying beliefs, and we all reap the results. As much as they might proclaim they have the nation/state/community's best interests at heart, the flip-flopping and changing course according to the latest or loudest voice would suggest that many politicians, particularly in the West, are more concerned about keeping their career in politics alive and holding on to power than the true good of their communities.

So what is the answer?

I believe it all comes back to our foundations. Thinking of our buildings, we want them straight, precise and on bedrock, not leaning to the left or right, not built in marshy or unstable land. It doesn't take much error in building foundations to end up with an unsafe, unstable structure. The same is true for our culture.

What are the foundations our culture is built on and are they adequate and sufficient to maintain a stable society?

Any structure must be built from the foundations up. Without knowing what the final product will look like, it is very difficult to determine what foundations are necessary. Just as problematic, if we decide to change the structure after laying the foundations, there is no guarantee the original foundations will be adequate for stability and durability. So it is with our culture and society. As we continue to change many aspects of the structure of our society, can we be sure that previous foundations are still appropriate? Will they keep us secure, or will they cause us to tumble? Can those foundations support our new structure? And that is before we have decided that we don't actually like many of those foundations and busily dig them up or otherwise destabilise them by pulling out or destroying the bits we don't like.

It is from this perspective that I will endeavour to return to our roots and some of those foundational beliefs to explore what needs assessment and even renovation or redesign for our survival.

In the beginning

"Did God really say…?"

The dilemma of choice goes back as far as history. And the choices we make depend on a myriad of factors. Personality and wiring, appetite, availability, culture, morality, our beliefs — about ourselves, our place in the world, how we deem the world to work, just to begin with. All these and more will impact the choices we make. However, even though the ability to choose is inherent, with all our education, understanding and abundance, the choices we might make and our capacity to follow through on the consequences of those choices are usually no less challenging. In fact, the abundance of choice may well make life more challenging.

Major aspects influencing the decisions we make rest on the information we have access to regarding the cost-benefit ratio of our decisions.

Who do we believe, and why?
What do we believe, and why?

There is an inextricable link between these two questions and how we answer them, particularly digging into the why part, not just at surface level, but like the proverbial three year-old, continuing to ask "but why?" until we are truly satisfied we have found the bedrock of our motivations and reasons. The answers to these questions impact every outcome and process of our lives. We really cannot afford to ignore them, to live as if it is okay to rely on our feelings in the moment even though many of us do. And when we do, the consequences have the potential to be dire. In response, I suggest most of the answers to these questions are connected to our perception of safety, protection and comfort and give us insight into what we truly value.

When trying to understand our world and our experiences, including our origins and purpose, the position we start from will greatly influence where we land. That is, what we already believe and our past experiences will leave us with an overt or perhaps more likely, subconscious set of beliefs underpinning the direction we head and the foundations we build on. Mostly, our tendency is to start from where we are and try to explain or understand the point of origin or foundational beliefs from what we see and know now. The problem is this leaves us with many paths to track back down. How do we know we will arrive at the right beginning? It would be like looking at someone standing in the centre of a city and deciding where they came from, or even by what transport they arrived. Sure, I can get some clues perhaps by the way they dress, the language they speak or any number of other indicators, but my assumptions may or may not be true.

This is one of the problems I see when people try to explain or deny God. While there is value in looking at behaviours and beliefs that are common across cultures, we still start from a position of seeing things from our human perspective rather than from God's. And that leads us to the question of how we can possibly see the world from God's perspective.

While answers might lie in ancient texts and scriptures, unfortunately, many people dismiss the Bible in particular because they believe it is a book of rules, or even about an angry, vengeful god, rather than realising the greater purpose is to give us insight into God and the relationship He wants to have with people.

Regrettably, even when they do read the Bible in order to gain insight into God, there is an additional tendency to pick out certain parts and decide this is an accurate picture of who He is. Like the story of the blind men describing an elephant as what they felt when they touched one part, we can do the same regarding God when we use examples divorced from any context or time period.

This is nothing new. In fact, one of the first events in the Biblical narrative is that the people God created believed a lie rather than what God had told them. The subtle miss-truth fed to them by the serpent was that rather than causing death, the fruit of the tree of the knowledge of good and evil would open their eyes and make them like God (Genesis 3:4,5), and they swallowed it without hesitation.

We see this theme echoed through a number of stories in the Bible, and in various cultures in the world. The tower of Babel is another example. Building a tower to heaven may be seen as another attempt to be like God. The underlying belief is that we don't need God; we can do it ourselves. I would not be the first to observe that science may just be our latest "tower of Babel" with the underlying assumption that "If we all work together we can find the answers to all the problems in the world without needing to refer to God". This brings us to the question many ask:

Why do we need God at all?

And closely related to this question is:

If we do need God, what should or does God look like?

What if we have it all wrong?

There are a number of observations I make as I view the world I live in alongside the news and media reports about it. So much of what we see and hear relates to how our world supposedly operates and what we must do to keep it going as such. However, for quite some time now, I have wondered if the "way the world works and must continue for us to survive", as told by those supposedly in the know, is actually just one big lie or deception, or perhaps worse, a series of partial truths. As I finish this book during the COVID-19 pandemic, the questions around this have become even more divisive.

But don't get me wrong. I am no conspiracy theorist, although at times I wonder...

Nevertheless, I do think that we could have it all wrong. However, I am also generous enough to give credence to the idea that those who are true believers in what they see as the way the world works may be more deluded than malicious. They truly believe that the world must operate in this way because they have no vision of an alternative.

And this brings me to a big question:

What if there was a vision for an alternative?

Part of the problem as I see it is that many powerful, wealthy people have a great deal invested in the world operating the way it does. Whether it is because of their financial investments, from clothing manufacturing to the production of technology and other goods, or the actual structure of economy and government, those in positions of power, either through wealth or position (usually both) generally have no interest in major change. This model has made them very comfortable. A large proportion of those who live in the West also benefit immensely from this. Many have reflected more recently that the vast majority of people, at least in the West, live lives immensely more comfortable and safe than Kings did a couple of hundred years back. However, there is a rising tide of awareness that our comfort has been, and continues to be, generated on the back of the extreme discomfort and exploitation of a great number of other people. At some point, there will come a reckoning.

A recurring theme in fiction over the few decades or so is a genre termed teen dystopia. The common element in these movies and books is the picture of a world resulting from the failure of our current culture. Some disaster has arisen and destroyed most of the world — all that we know and hold dear — and those left have decided to start a new world order where such things will supposedly never occur again. They are determined to put processes and protections in place to prevent future declines into anarchy, which involve heavy constraints on how people are allowed to live, with an emphasis on order and the rigid adherence to social mores.

One such movie is *The Giver*. In this story, the elders mandated the role of each young person in society as they turned eighteen. In order to constantly feel good and be compliant, without any need or desire to question, the authorities enforced the use of medication to produce calm and tranquillity. Without giving too much away, one young person begins to question all this and starts to experience freedom and the fullness of life, which includes death and pain as well. From here, he questions the principles of the society he lives in, longing for freedom for everyone from the constrictions emanating from these ideals.

This is not a new concept. The social revolution of the 1960s and 1970s was also about breaking free from the restraints and expectations of orderly society, to create social acceptance of differences, and to allow people to express who they really felt they were without fear of ostracism or rejection. In many ways, we live in the result of that. And although in many respects we do seem to have more freedom to act as we please when we please, alongside this we are seeing glimpses of growing chaos and dysfunction. As much as we had a society where racial hatred was rife and there were other areas where elements of society were suppressed or disempowered, our greater freedom does not seem to have remedied the situation at all. In fact, division, hatred and intolerance of others' differences seems to have intensified and escalated in more recent years.

The problem is that complete freedom doesn't always lead to satisfaction. This is particularly true for those who are on the lower levels of the ladder and do not have access to the same perceived freedoms due to lack of finances, education, support and understanding. Although our media, television shows and movies often draw a picture of the happily-ever-after for everyone, especially those supposedly at the bottom of the heap, this is not the reality most people in those situations experience. Having worked with and in the environment of those from lower socio-economic backgrounds, the opportunities for change are generally not there. Most are trapped in a downward spiralling cycle, with each ensuing generation worse off than the last unless they have the good fortune to gain the support to get a leg up, not to mention having the vision to believe life could be different for them. However, even then, breaking free from the mindsets and beliefs that have held them captive for generations is not easy.

By way of contrast, from my observations and consideration of statistics[1], I also wonder if many young people today struggle with having so many choices. Growing up with the idea they can *do anything* and *be anything* is a huge open-ended responsibility that becomes a suffocating burden.

What if I make a mistake?

What if I ruin my life?

What if I fail?

The lack of boundaries or truly helpful, supportive guidance results in either a lack of decision-making or waiting so long for the perfect position or opportunity that the individual ends up doing nothing. It either becomes too hard to choose, or they are not prepared to do anything that looks even remotely different to "the dream".

I also wonder if everything from material goods to opportunities has come too easily, (whatever that might mean), we fail to develop good character and integrity? In previous generations, children had to do many chores and help in the family and beyond out of necessity. With less automated machinery, and pre-prepared goods, the daily activities of cleaning and food preparation took longer and often more hands. Pre-prepared foods were not available, so families made much from scratch or even grew their own.

As young child, I have memories of hot summer days spent in the kitchen mincing and cutting up fruit (all by hand) for jamming and bottling. We never bought jam or tinned fruit. Preserves were a way to have fruit in winter and a good use of the glut of fruit that would otherwise go to waste. These days, fruit and vegetables are flown in from other regions — even from the other side of the planet — so we can eat them all year round. Much of what people eat is no longer fresh in any sense of the word, often processed beyond recognition. Most people in the past wore at least some homemade clothing. Many toys and other household items were also homemade. All these things took time, but also gave a sense of value to possessions. Very little came without effort on behalf of someone connected to the recipient. People saw and felt the energy required to give them the life they had. Appreciation and gratitude were possibly more common. Anecdotally, talking to our adult children more recently, they are certainly very aware of this with the overabundance given to their children by extended family. There is a very clear subsequent disinterest and lack of enjoyment toward what is given on occasions such as birthdays and Christmas particularly. Gifts become a burden rather than a joy.

Today, many children in the West grow up with few expectations on their time and relatively few hardships, especially around food, clothing and material goods. Because of this, there is a great deal more freedom to do as they please. The necessity of physical hard work and the greater cost of goods in previous generations had the potential to naturally strengthen and develop character. People had to metaphorically keep swimming, or they quickly drowned. "If you don't work, you don't eat" was often quite literally true. As we have generally become more prosperous as a nation (particularly in Australia), the expectations of ease and comfort have become more prevalent, leading to the belief, as mentioned before, that we can do as we like. We don't believe we should have to conform to anyone else's values but our own, as poorly formed, thought out or acknowledged they might be. And so, without constraints or boundaries, we flip-flop between beliefs, ideas and practices, landing nowhere well. Anything goes and we follow. Far from being free, we have become enslaved to the next best thing. Rather than being educated people who think for themselves, take responsibility for themselves, practice self-control, self-discipline, we follow after whatever the latest celebrity or influencer[2] tells us will change our lives for the better. Our own personal experience is not valued as much as what someone else tells us is truth.

Reflecting on an advertisement I saw at my local gym for a race up the 88 floors of the Eureka Tower, I observed the outworking of this. What makes people so passionate about these sorts of activities? What makes it seem such a lofty and worthy goal? What achievement or outcome are they looking for? I came to the conclusion that there may be two aspects. It may be that people are looking for a challenge to meet; some sort of personal goal; to have something they can value to work towards in the face of a lack of challenge elsewhere. Another thought is related and is perhaps the kudos of participating or even placing in such an event. A comment made about the rising generation is that they are looking for notoriety, their few minutes of fame; there is a longing for others to just notice them. They are looking for validation of their existence.

My observation is that we badly need to reassess what we are doing here on this planet. Why are we here and what is our purpose? Although these are not new questions by any means, I wonder if perhaps they need to be re-explored for the current generations.

> **Why do we do the things we do? So many are a means to an end. To what end are we looking, and will our actions and plans really get us there**

Exploring human supremacy

I would guess that few, if any, from scientific or evolutionist backgrounds would say outright that they believe that humans are the supreme beings on our planet. And of course, it would depend on what measures one uses to determine that supremacy — is it intelligence[3] or the capacity to reason? Or even the ability to survive in adverse conditions? Many of these sorts of measures have a high level of subjectivity. However, whether we acknowledge it or not, the premise underlying most of our actions and studies is that we are, to all intents and purposes the highest life form on Earth.

If we didn't believe this, we would need to find someone or something else to consult. As we know, many people, both now and throughout the ages have done exactly this, consulting stars, tea leaves or other signs from beyond, or looking to a variety of gods or other spiritual entities for the answers they seek.

Of course, some would also say that we can learn a great deal from other organisms and their adaptations, and certainly these observations tell us much — perhaps more about their Creator, the Mind behind them than we are willing to acknowledge.

Many Christians, Jews and Muslims do overtly believe that humans are the supreme beings of creation. The understanding about God creating humans in His image and giving them dominion over the earth, second only to Him is a central tenet. Unfortunately, the problem with this concept is that our understanding of dominion is messy and often unhelpful.

All too often our idea of dominion has become self-serving, all about my personal power and freedom to do as I please, whether I have any opinion about God or not. This attitude has the potential to be extremely destructive. For hundreds of years it has underpinned the justification of the rape and pillage of our planet, along with the subjugation of any culture or people group deemed less advanced or more pagan than our own.

That aside, there is a veiled or passive belief in most of society that the world is all about us as humans, and maybe even more deep-rooted, it is all about me. But how did we get here, both to this planet and to this time, place and understanding? And if we believe change is necessary, how do we move on and get others to move with us? While we may disagree about our purpose, few would disagree that the outcome for our planet is looking pretty bleak on a number of fronts.

Returning to where I began, we all develop a set of fundamental beliefs about how the world works. They are not necessarily innate, but generally taught and modelled by those around us from pre-birth. It is not only the cultural environment, but the emotional and psychological environment we enter into. Studies have shown a correlation between the mother's mental health, attitudes and behaviours during pregnancy and outcomes for the baby. There are strong indicators these will impact the way a child will view and interact with the world from birth and beyond[4]. Other conditions and circumstances in early life equally impact what we view and accept as normal.

An anecdotal example comes from my own life. It wasn't until God supernaturally healed me from anxiety that I realised that everyone didn't feel that way or function from that place. I have wondered how much of this came about through the circumstances surrounding my birth.

Well before mobile phones, my parents were dairy farmers. I was child number three and on the way to the hospital for my birth, at around three in the morning, the car broke down far from anywhere. While my father went to find help, my mother was alone in the car and in the dark. When they finally arrived at the hospital, I was born within about half an hour. I can only imagine the level of anxiety my mother was feeling alone in that car. Being a nurse as well as giving birth to two previous children, she would have been well aware of how imminent my birth was and probably wondering if she would have to deliver the baby alone in the car! How much that impacted my anxiety hormones and receptors or to what extent this was spiritual I don't know. However, it is well within the realms of possibility that this had a major influence on my disposition.

Added to what we absorb from our family and culture of origin, the society we grow up in also has multiple sets of beliefs and rules around how the world works. We often receive these non-verbally; they can be so innate and prevalent that most people don't even question their validity or truth. They become accepted norms and stereotypes and it is hard to imagine there being any other idea of "truth" or "reality". So much of our experience and understanding has grown out of these perceived truths and realities. In turn, these truths and realities have been further validated by those experiences. These sorts of questions and reflections are the basis for philosophy, which asks, amongst other questions: "What is truth?" "What is real?"

I believe that how we answer these questions, or what we believe about the answers we are presented with, must be the starting point for discussion. Unless we have some foundational idea of the questions to ask, let alone the answers, we really have no understanding of what we are building on.

So just what are our beliefs built on?

To explain further, when I was studying science, our teachers instructed us that observation and experience are the building blocks for theory and practice. Theories are usually the outworking of observations and trial and error over a long period of time, most often more than one lifetime. Therefore, it takes a great deal to change an established theory. We tend to think or accept that because people widely believe it, because it seems to work, because it is useful, a theory must, in fact, be true.

We only need look at the way in which our schools teach the theory of evolution. Rather than presenting it as theory, almost everyone discusses it as fact. Pre-schoolers have these ideas instilled through children's television programs, movies, the toy industry and more. It is one of the most pervasive teachings after language and mathematics.

As a chemistry teacher, though, I taught the relative theories as just that: theories. I find it interesting (to say the least) that we now have at least two or three generations who see the theory of evolution as a fact. Even writing this, questioning the validity of this theory will likely have some questioning my intelligence or worse. There are a number of topics today where it is no longer safe or comfortable to question; where taking a different path to the accepted norm or so-called truth leaves one exposed and open to ridicule, if not vitriol and hatred. This leads to the questions:

What is truth and what is acceptable as truth? How do we measure it or decide? And who gets to decide?

Exploring truth

There is an intense challenge to the concept of truth occurring on a number of fronts in our current generation. In fact, many would declare we are now living in a post-modern, post-colonial and even post-truth era. In an age where information is quite literally at our fingertips, we are less and less certain about the reality or truth of any information we might find. Who can untangle the web of fake news, fake fake news and downright manipulation, lies and deceit? Being aware of the fact that even some twenty years ago, questions and answers were cut and pasted in a different order to the live interview by television news producers, it has become very difficult to know who and what to trust.

On top of these issues are the beliefs of some that the truth is what I decide it is. A couple of decades ago I was teaching in secondary school. On yard duty one day I noticed a student drop their rubbish. Approaching this student, I suggested they might like to pick up said rubbish and put it in the bin. The response? "That's not mine - I didn't drop it." This comment and others like it led to something of an ongoing joke among staff of "You didn't see me, you can't prove it, I didn't do it" as the stock response from students. The disturbing aspect was that observing these children, we realised that they actually believed what they said. It was as though they had a deep core belief that if they said something often enough and loud enough it would make it true. Even faced with evidence to the contrary, they were still in denial. In the intervening decades, this belief system seems to only have become more entrenched. Although there is no evidence of correlation here, the rise of narcissism and the associated lowering of empathy would tend to lend weight to the idea that telling the truth is an optional extra in subsequent generations. Along with this, I think that as we have moved away from the ability, or desire, of parents and teachers to mete out meaningful, or otherwise consequences for such behaviour, leading to a lack of boundaries in this and other areas. The final article cited here investigates the phenomena of people believing falsehoods after hearing them repeatedly. This lends weight to the idea that if I get away with telling lies enough times, then I will keep doing it.[5]

However, the question of what is true, what is real and even what is valid is not a new thought.

Over the millennia, our records of history would show that many before us have raised similar queries. While it is not the purpose of this book to be a study of philosophy through the ages, we cannot do justice to the concept of what constitutes truth and lies without reflecting on the journey of the people before us. We cannot arrogantly dismiss previous thoughts, examinations or dissections on this topic without running the risk of simply repeating history, or even missing important perspective. It is also crucial in this discussion to have some sort of definition of what is meant by truth and why truth is important.

On a very broad level, the idea of truth and reality are based on those things that we determine are knowable, or measurable; things that can be objectively and quantitatively known, that are not subject to personal perspective or belief. In the past few hundreds of years, this has often come down to the physical world: that which we can see, touch, smell, hear or taste. However, as science has delved deeper, the realisation that this is very limiting has led to a wider understanding or belief about truth. The discovery and study of phenomena unseen, assumed unmeasurable (by traditional measures) and unobservable with the human senses seems to push the boundaries of reality and truth into ever expanding universes, or dare I say, multiverses.

In our post-modern society, beyond the realm of scientists and physicists, there seems to be an increasing belief that truth can be very subjective: what is true for you is not necessarily true for me. Alongside this statement is the premise that this is acceptable. Unfortunately, this only seems to work as far as your idea of truth doesn't impinge, negate or otherwise collide with mine!

Historically, as mentioned, theories about truth had their basis in fact: what is knowable, or measurable. However, even within this, there are different ways of thinking about truth. On the one hand, some would argue that there is one absolute truth that leads to a coherent whole. Others would argue that there are many smaller truths, that may or may not be related to or even dependent upon each other.

There are a number of differing theories about how we determine whether something is true. For example, correspondence theory considers something true if it has consistent measurable, observable facts. Alternatively, coherence theory, considers a belief true only as far as it is part of a logical, rational system of beliefs. Pragmatic theories of truth suggest that beliefs must fit in with experience, past and present. Perhaps the best way to look at truth is a mix of these or perhaps we see it as dependent on which realm — physical, emotional, spiritual — we are looking at.

Throughout history, though, an underlying pride in and belief of the importance of human achievement would seem to run concurrently with all these theories about truth. I see this as being quite central to the way we view ourselves and our place in the world. It underlies and undergirds all these ideas about truth at some level. Without a different worldview, it is very difficult to escape the interaction. We measure, quantify and qualify all we think and believe through the lens of our centrality as humans. We are at once limited and constrained by our own views, experience, understanding and even our language, preventing us from stepping outside to see from a different vantage point.

There is a level at which I find this amusing. Inasmuch as we have educated our children to believe that they are simply a cosmic accident and (perhaps) the highest level of evolution so far (although some would disagree, especially those living with cats!), we still have a great deal of conceit about our abilities within this space. It is as though we think that it is our efforts, our brilliance, our intelligence, which have brought us to this point. (Except, of course, for those "idiots" who started the industrial revolution and the proceeding generations who have destroyed the planet for those coming!)

And then we talk about the giftedness of individuals. But if our abilities, talents and intelligence are a gift, where did those gifts come from? Who was the giver? We like to depersonalise (or otherwise deflect) the answer to something like Mother Nature, without acknowledging that this is really just another name for a god — someone outside our realm who exists on another plane, with other special powers.

In more recent history, however, the battle for truth would appear to be coming to a head. In the last few hundred years, the changes to human activity and technology seem to be on a cumulative trajectory. The industrial age of only some two hundred years past was a period when the combustion engine transformed the world as people knew it in all arenas of life. Transport and manufacturing were major areas where life sped up. Instead of taking a day to go from one town to another, we could cross a country. A trip across the world that took six to eight months under sail lasted the same number of weeks on a steamer, and eventually down to hours with the development of flight. Production of goods previously manufactured completely by hand became mechanised, greatly increasing the volume of products available while decreasing the price. Life changed drastically. This was the beginning of the so-called modern era.

Preceding and overlapping this time, a number of countries employed the concept of colonialism to extend their authority over other people and territories. The paradigm of terra nullius — the belief that if no supposedly civilised peoples lived there, the *land belonged to no one* — was the underlying justification. This generally included the aim of developing and exploiting these territories to their own benefit.[6]

In the last few decades, there has been a great deal of criticism of this approach and behaviour. Destructive aspects to both the original inhabitants and the physical land have become very apparent. Unfortunately, there are so many ways in which the global village is now the reality we live in. It is impossible to go back and separate any place on the planet (and likely beyond, given the prevalence of space junk!) from the influence of the West. Numbers of those in the two-thirds of the world not considered part of the West have mobile phones before the luxury of running water. This is no joke! We have travelled in a number of countries, from Russia (to Indonesia and Uganda, where this was literally the truth. A great many people living in places with no access to running water seemed to have mobile phones, even as far back as the mid 2000s.

In the midst of these two aspects of global expansion — the Industrial Revolution and Colonialism — was the growth of science. Universities became more prevalent and as places for the discussion, expansion and testing of ideas, and also became increasingly secular and removed from the control and administration by the Church than they had been in the past. Rising out of philosophy, this thirst for knowledge set the scene for the development of the sciences as we know them today.

In the desire to understand and make the most of all the world and universe has to offer, the schools of physics, chemistry and biology took on a life of their own. The draw and power of the promise of ultimate truth and reality was so attractive that these appropriated a godlike status in society. With an emphasis on procedure and evidence-based thinking, it was anticipated science would offer all the answers those disillusioned, disappointed and failed by religion were looking for. Our desire for control, through understanding and knowledge, would finally be satisfied. The quintessential question of the meaning of "life, the universe and everything" promised to find its answers within these constructs. (And, no, it wasn't going to be as simple as 42![7])

However, escape from the constraints of religion is not a new way of thinking. If we have any regard for the Bible, the idea of a society without the need for God or religion has been around for many thousands of years. It is not a deep dig into the stories of the Old Testament to see that this is one of the main struggles illustrated throughout: the desire of people to live without God, or to make god(s) that would serve their own purposes and desires. In our post-modernity, we just don't realise this is what we are doing!

As I intimated earlier, underlying all this is the desire to be in control, to be the top of the heap when it comes to predicting or even manipulating outcomes for every circumstance in life. Indeed, we see this clearly illustrated way back in the first part of Genesis chapter eleven, when people decided to claim an identity through the building of a tower. With some background understanding it seems likely they were following their desire to find their identity apart from relationship with God. The desire for the perceived freedom from accountability was perhaps a major driver.

The Biblical narrative informs us that at this stage, God put a blockage in front of them through the scrambling of language and so the place became known as Babel. The translation of this word is confusion. It is an interesting reflection that while they were trying to escape the confusion, fear of dispersal and the loss of their identity, that was exactly where they ended up as they chased something other than God. Perhaps not too much has changed since then.

In trying to determine what truth is, unless we find a reference point, it is quite difficult to nail anything down. Philosophers grappled with this question through the ages and Descartes illustrated the struggle well with his famous answer to the search for an irrefutable statement; one that could have no argument against it. The idea that "I think, therefore I am"; that my own existence is the only thing I can be sure of, may seem a little pointless or even stupid to many. Of course, far more exists than me – I experience it. However, the question Descartes was possibly asking is, "how can we tell that what we experience is the same?"

My daughter and I were surprised by each other in a discussion where we revealed that we had both thought about this possibility. We had both had the thought that we cannot be sure we are experiencing the same thing as each other. We might use the same language to describe something that we both experience very differently. For example, I might look at a colour which I call blue. She might look at the same colour and call it blue. However, who knows whether what we see is the same? And right now, some reading this are asking the question, "why does it matter as long as you can communicate effectively?"

The idea in all this is that we need a reference point. And this is where we hit a blockage. Can we ever agree to the same point of reference and what it should be? If it is the ultimate supremacy of human beings, there are numerous flaws, some of which I have already mentioned. If we start to use a concept of God, then whose concept is correct? Whose concept is imaginary and whose is real? How do we know?

For me personally, I come back to my science roots. In science, theories emerge through trial and error — what seems to work with and match the evidence? What is it that doesn't work? Is there an experience or circumstance that doesn't match the theory? If these become unanswerable, or evidence surfaces that refutes the theory, then the theory requires modification or even abolition. Perhaps we view God as just one more theory.

In my own journey, I have stepped out in faith and begun to walk the path of believing in God as the Source of all life, understanding and meaning. The further I have gone, the more sense it has made. I have tentatively let go of my human understanding and what I have been taught about the origins of the universe by science. As I have exchanged these views for living, operating and transforming my beliefs in accordance with a Biblical perspective on these things, I have found those Biblical perspectives more and more believable. They have made more and more sense of what I observe and become more and more helpful in finding the answer for what I see as a world in increasing danger and chaos as we try to fix it ourselves. There is a point at which, while we continue to use the same thinking that got us in the mess we find ourselves in globally — the idea that human ingenuity and intelligence can fix every problem we have — we run the danger of simply digging the proverbial hole deeper.

From this perspective, the remainder of this book overtly explores the idea that there is a God who created this world, that He does have a plan for it and that we can work with Him to bring it all back into the good that He originally intended it to be. I will endeavour to unpack a variety of beliefs commonly held, illuminate some flaws in them and offer some alternative thoughts. Please come with me.

Exploring emotions and feelings

The story of what went wrong in the Garden of Eden as described in Genesis chapter three, illustrates a pattern of the temptation to follow our feelings and emotions complete with the subsequent impact this can have in our lives. To begin with Eve allowed her feelings to twist her away from what she had directly been told by God. First her adversary sowed doubt: "Did God really say…?" (Genesis 3:1). Next, came a distortion of what God had said: "You must not eat from any tree in the garden" as opposed to "You are free to eat from any tree in the garden; but you must not eat from the tree of the knowledge of good and evil" (Genesis 2:16-17). And then more feelings proceeded, particularly attraction, and she "saw…the fruit of the tree was good for food…pleasing to the eye…desirable for gaining wisdom" (Genesis 3:6). The consequences of surrendering to these feelings were the negative emotions of shame and fear: "…they hid from the Lord God…" (Genesis 3:8). Even though God had only shown them love and His goodness in the past, they exchanged the truth about God for a lie (Romans 1:25).

> *"They exchanged the truth about God for a lie, and worshipped and served created things rather than the Creator…"*

Some two hundred years ago, when knowledge and understanding of the world was exploding, emotions tended to be relegated to the backburner as unreliable, unpredictable, confusing, unknowable and generally unhelpful as the concept of fact ascended to the highest place of regard. In a predominantly male dominated society, emotions were seen as the realm of women and children, and as such, a lesser way of interacting with the world. Indeed, women who struggled with their emotions were often labelled neurotic or hysterical and locked away. Over time, we have continued to grapple with what to do with emotions we see as negative and troublesome. The amount of money and effort poured into adverstising and ongoing discussions to deal with and confront the shame and stigma associated with depression is a legacy of this. Added into this mix, the perception that being manly or masculine is congruent with a lack of emotional exhibition meant the men of previous generations often became quite emotionally detached: emotions were untrustworthy and could get you into trouble.

As an example, my father grew up in London during the second world war and he struggled to deal with his emotions to the end of his life. I believe he quite possibly had PTS (post traumatic stress). He and his mother and siblings lived separately to his father during the blitz on London and they never knew from day to day whether my grandfather was still alive. I guess in that scenario, you just have to get on with life. You can't stop and get bogged down with emotional responses or you end up incapacitated, so you need to lock them down. We see the same in the faces of children from current war situations. Looking at the deadness in their eyes, they appear to have completely emotionally shut down. The danger is that it may lead to a lack of compassion or empathy, and so you could become quite hardened and able to harm others without remorse, not to mention the impact of trauma that has not been dealt with on other aspects of emotional and physical health.

Traumatic situations such as these illustrate that rational thought doesn't solve every issue. The suppression of emotion actually does a great deal of damage. Realising the truth in this, at some point our society seems to have swung the pendulum in the opposite direction, though, moving to a position where we not only believe our emotions are important and we should listen to them, but more completely, that our emotional response gives us the answer or is the answer whenever we have a difficulty. The current position from some voices would seem to be that we should respond according to our emotions and do whatever they tell us to do, that our emotions tell us the truth about every scenario we encounter. Statements like "you make me angry/sad" also suggest that we don't believe we can control our emotional response. Further, others then become responsible for our emotional state. Some of our laws around offense add fuel to this belief as they seek to outlaw opinions, beliefs and conversation that might cause offense to certain groups.

Addressing the positive side of our emotions, and our perception of their desirability, the Dalai Lama comes to mind. For a religious figure, he seems to have had significant airtime. Watching an interview with him some time back, his parting wisdom for the question of what our purpose on earth is amounted to the words, "Be happy". While this possibly has some merit, it is difficult to understand how this relates to the millions living in abject poverty in our world, let alone those going through really difficult times. How do I actually enact being happy when I am feeling desperately miserable? And for those who have little to no control over any outcomes in their lives, this is far easier to say than to live. In many ways, it doesn't sound much different to the mantra of the 1970's: "If it feels good, do it". Simply sweep aside and ignore the other realities, experiences and practicalities of life and enjoy yourself, that is, until the failings of this mode of living lead to a crashing fall. This may be financially, relationally, or physically — when the money runs out, when our families and friends tire of bailing us out, or our bodies no longer cope with the abuse we have heaped on them.

A major issue I observe is that we live in a culture that has become very pain averse. There is an increasing breadth and availability of pharmaceuticals to fix every imaginable pain and an ever-expanding use of illicit drugs to make us feel good. Our lives often seem to revolve around the next feel good experience where anything that might prevent us enjoying every moment is to be mercilessly eradicated. I saw an illustration of this a number of years back, hearing a mother say to her son, who was on the verge of leaving his family for another woman, "do whatever makes you happy". There was no sarcasm in this statement, but permission. We hate to see people unhappy, especially those who are close to us. We just don't know how to handle negative emotions.

How are we to manage negative emotions?
What are they there for?

I believe many of us look to external mechanisms as the antidote to feeling bad. This can be anything from consumables and new gadgets to the next experience or relationship. We buy a bigger, newer car or house, (or get renovations to the existing one), a new tv or phone. We go on another trip, cruise, outing to see another part of the world or complete another experience on our bucket list. We seem to be endlessly chasing the next thing that will give us that feel good buzz. And unfortunately, there are many who encourage us by telling us how blessed, lucky, happy, wonderful, awesome and deserving we are to have these opportunities. And so, we feel even better because someone else envies what we have, rarely realising that we are just putting on another bandaid[8] and that the vacuum inside is increasingly expanding, threatening to overwhelm us.

As a parent, I have noted how pervasive this is in our child-rearing as well. We don't like to see our children unhappy or struggling so we often end up helping them to self-medicate on these same things. It starts small — our child is crying because they fell over and hurt themselves and we give them something sweet to take their mind off it. In effect, this is the beginning of our addiction. Feel pain — medicate it.

So what is the fundamental lie here?

We believe *"pain is bad and is to be avoided at all costs"*.

We believe that the emotions we view as negative are bad and avoidance of them at all costs is essential.

When I was studying psychology (at which time I was on medication for depression), one of my tutors was a professor of neuropsychology. He made a statement during one of our classes that, "one day there will be a happy pill and that everyone will be on it and we will all feel happy all the time". Of course, I felt the need to remind him what a lecturer had just told us, that no one had yet been able to differentiate between when an emotion occurred and the release of corresponding chemicals (neurotransmitters) in the brain. In a nutshell, there was no way to determine whether it was the release of these chemicals that caused the emotion or whether the emotion causes the release of the chemicals. Since then, further studies have revealed that these neurotransmitters are not only released in the brain, but in the heart and the gut.[9] This is another example of science catching up with what we innately know: "I just feel it in my gut", or "you warm/broke my heart". Our bodies tell us a great deal about our wellbeing or lack of it, but we don't always have the skills to correctly interpret just what it is they are saying.

This begs the question, then, what importance do negative and painful emotions have and subsequently, how are we to deal with them?

If we look into the purely physical world, we can see that pain is incredibly important. The physical pain receptors in our bodies tell us something is not right. One of the biggest problems for those suffering from a disease like leprosy is that their neural pathways and pain receptors are damaged. This results in a lack of awareness of injuries that are sustained, resulting in far greater damage occurring through infection and repeated damage. Significant burns, cuts and abrasions can go unnoticed until infection sets in, which in turn can even lead to the loss of body parts when pain, the early warning system, is not working.

In my mind, the issue surrounding leprosy in terms of the long term negative health outcomes gives a profound physical example or picture of the dangers of numbing ourselves emotionally and spiritually. All of these ultimately lead to death, either physical, spiritual or both.

We can have the same issues emotionally. And just like we want to eradicate the physical pain, either the symptoms or the issue

— we don't care — we do the same with emotional pain: just stop the pain, whatever the cost. Whether it fixes the underlying problem or not, we often simply treat the symptoms, not the cause. And because we have become so used to medicating ourselves out of those symptoms of emotional pain, it is not until we look properly in the mirror, or we experience the pain of our clothes not fitting, or our friends and family take us aside that we realise we have been emotionally binge eating again (that whole packet of mint slices in one sitting was always going to be a bad idea!), or whatever else it is we have been doing. And yes, some of our self-medication leads to much more pervasive problems than this. Addictions such as alcohol, drugs, gambling, sex, pornography, even spending, so often, if not always, have their roots in the desire to medicate against pain.[10]

Or perhaps it is through our intimate relationships. At the last night of a divorce recovery program I participated in, I found myself talking to a gentleman I had not really met before. He asked why I had come to the course? What had prompted me? The answer seemed pretty obvious to me. I didn't want to ever go through this pain again, so I was going to make sure I dealt with my stuff so I could at least recognise unhealthy in others. I then asked him the same and was quite gobsmacked at his response: "yeah, after three failed marriages, I thought I'd better do something about it". I didn't say it, but the thought fairly shouted through my brain: "it took you that long?"

We could use any relationships to medicate ourselves. However, this begs the question of why we are so afraid of being alone. This in itself could be a whole book and I'm sure someone has already written it! Having a relationship may give us the distraction from our pain that we are looking for, but why are we in pain?

What is the message we are believing about our isolation or loneliness, or even just "aloneness"?

Do we believe that our value only comes from being in a relationship? This was certainly something that was true for me. In my early twenties, I had a belief I didn't even admit to myself, that being married meant that at least someone wanted me. I felt, at least at some level, that I would find value and acceptance in a marriage relationship. Underlying these sorts of beliefs is another: do we actually believe that someone else can or should make us happy? This is another faulty belief that leads simply to a whole lot more pain as others' inability to meet our expectations impacts us again and again. What other lies are we believing about ourselves and our identity? (More on this in the next chapter.)

For others, we might use success, money or power as our medication. As long as we perceive ourselves as doing better financially or career-wise than our neighbour, we measure ourselves as ok. As long as I am top of the heap, as long as I am the boss of at least someone, (even if it is only the dog), I am doing ok. We might even do this vicariously through our children. From baby beauty pageants to every other competition for children, including education, until they grow up and have careers and their own beautiful, wonderful spouse, children and perfect life, we can use these as a measure of our success, our value, our performance as people. Just take a stroll through Facebook. It becomes blatantly obvious when you see the posts of people you know well, and all they ever post is the good news stories, while you know for a fact they are all but drowning in the aspects of life not going so well.

Sadly, it is often only when our expectations are failed in any of these arenas that we realise just how much we were relying on them to feel good, to be happy. How quickly do we lose our happiness as the circumstances of life either erode it or even suddenly shift so as to pull the proverbial rug from under our feet? Pain comes rushing in, in all its glorious power to overwhelm us with its bitterness. The COVID-19 global pandemic is an example of this on steroids. For so many of us, we seem to have lost much of what we thought gave us failsafe security, whether it was a career or even employment, the ability to do as we please when we want. Having been through the pain of divorce, one of the major losses for me at that time was the future that I had all mapped out, which relied on the presence of the other person. Just as I had to find a new future, many of us are also now in that place, where there is so much uncertainty about what is next. This can be a very painful place to live in.

There are so many gateways in our world to that which has potential to cause us emotional pain. Sometimes it is direct, in the form of some kind of loss or grief, either from physical removal of someone or something, or because what we expected did not occur. Sometimes it is because of our compassion, be that for other humans who are suffering, for animals or for the planet in general. In reality, it is inevitable that we will eventually feel pain of some kind. Even if we have had the most diligent helicopter parents, who have worked their hardest to protect us from any sort of pain, either from external sources or as a result of our own choices, one day pain will find us.

The methods we use to deal with pain — whether it is avoidance and medication, processing and understanding or anything between — will ultimately reflect our beliefs about ourselves and our place in the world. Emotional pain is particularly in the spotlight here as it tends to have so many more stigmas attached than physical pain.

In the main, the cause of physical pain is quite obvious and well accepted. If you have a car accident and break bones, whether it was through your own actions or another's, sympathy and compassion are generally available, as well as treatment. The emotional impact of this, or any other trauma, physical or not, is not so visible and not so easy to fix. Not only do we have less understanding of the mechanisms of emotions, but we have even less understanding of how to repair the damage, other than the proverbial "time heals all wounds". So we come back to the tried and tested medical model of healing that treats the symptoms to try to make the pain manageable, while desperately trying to find a cure. Or perhaps we just try to eliminate the possibility of experiencing pain through changing laws to prevent people doing anything that might cause them pain. And then we alter others laws because they might cause pain by suggesting there is something wrong with what we want to do.

However, the size of the problem is not getting smaller. As I observe the way in which the society I live in tries to fix the emotional pain of so many, it looks to me like trying to put a bandaid on a shark bite, or giving someone paracetamol for a broken leg. Many of our treatments barely touch the symptoms and any sort of cure we are hoping for seems totally disconnected from those treatments.

At a personal level, an example of this is the depression I suffered for a number of years after my marriage ended. While I do not claim that it was severe in comparison to others, I was on medication for about four years. The positive aspect of medication was that it stopped the depth of the pain and hopelessness; it smoothed the edges and lifted me to a place where I could function at a better level. (Which is what much of our medical model is about: enabling a person to continue to function at some level.) However, it had severe limitations. It was only after ceasing the medication that I realised the flattening effect it had on my emotions. It may have helped me not to spend so much time crying, but it also limited my enjoyment of life — there was not the sense of anticipation of good things or excitement and happiness in doing things that I would usually have enjoyed. It was not the medication that cured me. I do believe, though, it did help me to be in a position to enact and understand some things, such as how I got my energy replenished as an extrovert, and to be able to deal with other self-worth and identity issues that improved my wellbeing in the longer term. In the end, I believe God granted me significant healing in this, even though my doctor suggested I would have repeated bouts throughout my life. That episode is now over twenty years back, without recurrence.

As a society, it concerns me that even with our greater awareness and greater acceptance and compassion around emotional issues, the problems don't seem to have decresed. The rate of youth and young adult suicide continues to grow, despite increasing opportunities, increasing standards of living and increasing freedoms. For those aged 15-44 in Australia, it was the leading cause of death from at least 2014-2016 and this doesn't include those who attempted suicide or engaged in deliberate self-harm.[11]

While we can investigate the causes and cures or treatments continually, I can't help but wonder if there are a few factors involved that we don't really want to know about — factors that confront us with the reality of the lies we use to prop up our society and our way of life. Again, they require a reassessment of some of our fundamental beliefs and an adjustment to how we live life. Generally, we just don't want to go there, even if we do become aware. It's all too hard.

An observation from a young friend who came from Ghana, having never travelled before, was also quite enlightening. He commented that he had thought that when he came to Australia everyone would be really happy because they had everything they needed. He was surprised and shocked when he saw the levels of depression and misery in a place of such opulence compared to where he grew up. It was a quick lesson in the inability of stuff to make us happy.

※

But why are we so unhappy?

※

It is difficult to measure, but I would suggest we are also generally less happy than our parents and their parents before them, even though they had significantly less materially, and life would seem to have been tougher for them than it is for us. Many forget that back in the 1940s, during and after WW2, many commodities such as food, clothing and fuel were rationed, even here in Australia. In the UK rationing continued until 1954, nearly ten years after the war had ended. Many today would generally appear to be healthier, work less hours, have more holidays overseas and live longer, but, given the rising rates of anxiety and depression,[12] I am not sure we are as happy let alone happier.

I believe that there are several aspects to this problem.

One of the shifts I have seen over my lifetime is in our need to wait, or even work, for anything. A lightweight example of this is the fact that our shops start stocking hot cross buns and

Easter eggs quite soon after Christmas. More recently, it has become Boxing Day! As a child, we waited for hot cross buns until Good Friday and Easter eggs were for Easter Sunday. Now they are part of everyday life for some two or three months of the year. It is similar with many aspects of childhood. Items the last generation waited to receive as birthday and Christmas gifts are expected by the current generation as part of living a normal life. Much of that which we deemed special is now ordinary or an expected norm. I know of numbers of families who take regular overseas trips. In the past, it took a long time to save up the money to have these sorts of experiences and goods. As a child, we waited years before we got our first colour television and then it was second-hand. In Australia, our welfare system now deems this as a basic necessity and will supply you with one if you can't afford it.

And we have done the same with sex. Far from keeping a sexual relationship to one person within marriage, we use sex to validate ourselves, to feel good, to further medicate ourselves from our pain, or simply as recreation. Our society tells us that sexual activity is a normal part of life for anyone over about sixteen or even younger and as such, should be embraced.

The problem with the use of all of these to medicate ourselves is that although they might dull the senses for a time, eventually there is a reckoning. Just like any physical drug, over time we need to use more and more to give us the same high and all the time the side effects are continuing to impact our finances, our relationships, our physical health and over all wellbeing and they keep escalating. (As someone who is a self professed drug-addict, porn-addict, sex-addict and narcissist, Russell Brand is quite vocal about what he sees as the problems with these sorts of behaviours and the hopelessness embedded within them.[13])

Brené Brown[14] tells a story that well illustrates another aspect of our unhappiness. It is the story of the massive increase in depression in the women of a village after technology caught up and they all got washing machines. Previously, they met down at the river and laundry was a communal affair. Getting washing machines created a disconnect between them and instead of working together and helping each other, through relationship, they became isolated and independent. This is something so relevant in our lives now, where we have reduced so many of our connections to being across the digital divide of social media. Rather than giving us greater connectedness, these have often increased our sense of loneliness and isolation.

In *Surprised by Joy*, C.S. Lewis also describes the impact of our technology and bus-y-ness well, even though he wrote this many years ago when much of what we take for granted was not imagined. Reflecting on his own childhood, he said,

> *"The deadly power of rushing about wherever I pleased had not been given me. I measured distances by the standard of man, man walking on his two feet, not by the standard of the internal combustion engine. I had not been allowed to deflower the very idea of distance; in return I possessed "infinite riches" in what would have been to motorists "a little room". The truest and most horrible claim made for modern transport is that it "annihilates space". It does. It annihilates one of the most glorious gifts we have been given. It is a vile inflation which lowers the value of distance, so that a modern boy travels a hundred miles with less sense of liberation and pilgrimage and adventure than his grandfather got from ten. Of course if a man hates space and*

> *wants it to be annihilated, that is another matter. Why not creep into his coffin at once? There is little enough space there."*

In our desire for instant gratification and less work, I can't help but wonder whether we have made our own misery. Some seventy years on from Lewis, space in our lives has become premium.

On a recent trip to the central business district of our capital city, I was reflecting to my husband on the exorbitant and totally unwarrantable price of parking, particularly overnight. His response was exactly that: "space is at a premium". Living on the semi-rural fringe of suburbia, we regularly appreciate the depth of view we have out across the mountains and valleys. As we experienced many weeks of not being allowed to travel more than five kilometres from home due to lengthy lockdowns, this became even more valued. I cannot imagine the pressure of those weeks without being able to get out for more than a couple of hours a day for those living in inner suburbia, sometimes without even having a yard. However, I do believe the weeks spent without work, sport and other relentless activity have also raised a greater appreciation for space in our lives, both physical and mental. Without the long commutes and incessant taxiing of children to activites, numbers of people have recognised the positive effects of the increased space for rest in their daily schedules.

Studying for my master's degree, our lecturer constantly referred back to the idea that God creates space for life. It would appear one silver lining of lockdown may be we are rediscovering that empty space, of both time and territory, far from being scary and intimidating, are perhaps the place where joy and freedom abound — the place where we find what life is really about.

Exploring my value

Underlying much of our unhappiness, lack of satisfaction and need to medicate our pain away is the question of who we are and why (or even if) we and our lives matter. For the last few generations, we have grown up with the concept that we can be and do whatever we want to, if we just try hard enough!

In a health magazine, I came across the statement, *"Whatever the mind can conceive and believe, the mind can achieve"*.[15] Science would back this up with the discovery that what we think or believe can actually change aspects of our DNA.[16] And of course, we have known the power of negative thoughts over our behaviour and outcomes for a long time. If I believe I am useless, stupid or not able to do something, most of the time my actions will tend to reinforce this, subsequently reinforcing the negative belief and so on in a downward spiral. We have often had people around us lend their support to these beliefs as well, with their words and actions toward us. As a secondary school teacher, I observed this across generations in families, where the beliefs about themselves were continuously perpetuated and reinforced. In many ways it shows up on both sides of the divide, were the proverbial "rich get richer".

But for many of us, we have tried to be something different, to be someone different, to change our behaviours and interactions to no avail. We have not been able to change our negative attitudes or beliefs about ourselves by simply enacting our will. We can't even lose a few kilos of weight, stick to a diet or exercise plan. If we could, we wouldn't need the plethora of gyms and weight loss methodologies cramming our suburbs and browsers.

Fundamental to the fact that it is very difficult to really change ourselves is the question of whether we need to. We build our view of ourselves on our beliefs about who we are — our value, our worth and our identity. As much as some do grow up being told how special, valuable and wonderful they are, there is a point at which most of us question the truth of this, especially when we experience rejection or failure: What is it that makes me intrinsically special or wonderful?

At odds with this model of teaching and encouraging our children, and in direct opposition to these beliefs, we then teach them that they are simply a cosmic accident brought about by evolution. There is no real purpose to them or our world. It just happened to come into being. Of course, this also leads to a great deal of other conflicting questions, including why we are so concerned about extinction of species and global climate change and the like, if everything is simply on a course set in motion by some sort of big bang or other chance happening. If that includes the human race, then by extension, it must include everything we do.

Without some sort of identity or purpose to our being here, it is very easy to fall into a negative state of mind. Of course, many people will find their identity and purpose through their family and friends, through work or other activities that somehow give meaning and direction to life. The problem occurs, though, when we lose one or more of these, usually through no choice of our own. If I no longer have a position of power, or some event, or other people hurt the good name of my family, or I lose my money, my friends or both, what is it that defines me and gives me purpose? And to what end? If life is just for the enjoyment of this moment, it does a pretty shoddy job of it for many people around the globe. This observation is not at all new and is reflected in Ecclesiates 1:2, where the writer laments, ""Meaningless! Meaningless!...Utterly meaningless! Everything is meaningless.""

Again, we can allow the media and others to tell us what our meaning and purpose should look like, but for many of us, eventually we come to a place where we start to see the hollowness and superficiality of most of this. Even the most diligent work in humanitarian good deeds can be disillusioning when we see those executing these deeds simply looking for power, money or a good name (fame). All the altruism in the world needs to come with the question: How does it stop being about me and my validation of self as worthy and good? (There are so many examples of this in so called mission work, where what is supplied is far more about the supplier and what they would like to do than about what is actually needed.[17])

And then, as we look around and wonder why we do much of what we do, it creates another problem. We cook, clean, eat, work just to do it all again tomorrow and the next day and the day after that. If it is all simply for what happens in this brief life, why does much of it matter? If it is all simply about this life, why do we care so much? If we are all a product of evolution, then who we are and what we do has very little significance, unless we believe that by some fluke, we are the ones that are going to halt the progress of evolution or improve on it.

But of course, we are not satisfied with little significance. I am amazed by the amount of time spent by teen girls particularly, (but I am sure it relates to many others in a slightly different form), in marketing their personal brand. In the few short years since the advent of the smart phone, this phenomenon has taken over the lives of numbers of people. We believe that everything put out into the digital public domain has an impact on our image, value and worth according to the numbers of likes and followers. It doesn't matter how much of the material is true, accurate or doctored. It is all about how it appears to others. And just as devastating, if someone takes a dislike to you, they have an extraordinary amount of power to destroy your online image, leaving you bereft and isolated socially, emotionally and sometimes even financially.

Looking at the statistics, even with all this interaction and opportunities, we seem to be lonelier and more unhappy with ourselves.[18] Our desire to be progressive — moving forward from all those aspects of our society we have deemed inappropriate or unhelpful to us — all seems to be wrapped up in the idea of fulfillment and freedom to be all that we possibly can; to rise to the highest level.

In psychology, this has been labelled as self-determination or self-identification, but these terms have migrated into the general populace in our attitudes and beliefs at least. We have the desire to be free to decide for ourselves every aspect of who we are, even to the point of denying physical attributes and the reflection of not only the mirror, but those around us. While we might defend our right to choose who we are in every way, the issues this causes us in our relationships with others and the world around us are escalating. And while we might adulate the individual as the one who knows best who they are, anyone who has raised children knows how quickly these ideas change. In the end, there is little stability or boundaries to give any sort of security or measure. The extrapolation of this is that there is no longer a base line or foundational starting point to any sense of self, leaving the individual floating in free fall in space, with no tether to anything.

Exploring freedom

One of the big pushes coming out of the 1960s and 70s was around the concept of freedom. The song by Marlo Thomas, *Free to be…you and me* comes to mind. The driving desire was to break free from any inhibiting social mores deemed an impediment to personal fulfillment. This included everything from hairstyles (it was short hair for men and long hair for women) and clothing to sexual relationships and the sort of work we might do in order to be socially acceptable. People wanted to escape the pressure of performing to the beat of someone else's drum and the stereotypes they saw dictating their lives.

One of the greatest issues with personal freedom, though, is how to prevent my freedom from impinging on your freedom. An illustration that comes to mind is around the idea of privacy.

In our school system, we had parents who were so protective of their rights to privacy that they would not have their children checked for head lice. Even if the teacher could see lice on a child's head, rules had been put in place to prevent them talking to the parents about it. The only way in which a teacher could approach the issue of head lice was via an opt-in offer for a head check by a school nurse. Unfortunately, some parents refused to opt-in, and these were often ended up being the parents of children who had lice. The escalating problem left other parents in the state of continually dealing with head lice in their own children because others refused to. Their right to privacy and freedom not to deal with a problem clearly impinged on a number of other children and parents' rights to be lice free. However, as ridiculous as it might sound, teachers and parents seemed powerless to do anything about it.

Even as I spent time writing this book in my local public library, the outworking of our craving for freedom has made itself known to me. Watching the behaviour of teens towards each other in and around public spaces seems immensely different to a generation ago. There appears to be little respect for others — both those working in the space, as well as their friends and peers. Looking at the statistics and issues around their behaviour on social media, we could equally presume they have just as little respect for one another and themselves, given some of the explicit material they share and consume. I have also been surprised by the number of people who don't have their phones on silent and then hold conversations at full volume (both on the phone and with others) in the library. Public transport seems to be the same.

As a teacher and parent, I have been quite dismayed at the lack of what I would deem appropriate boundaries for children. Even some twenty years ago, I had students who held a party for some seventy other students while their parents where away.

The house was trashed. What amazed me further was that this was not the first time this had happened and there seemed to be few consequences. However much previous generations may have felt constrained and hemmed in by pressures to conform and follow prescribed paths, the shift to conforming to peers and the lack of clear boundaries and any sort of direction and guidance would appear to leave the current generations feeling unsafe, uncertain and without purpose. If you have any doubt about this, just take a look at our suicide, anxiety and depression statistics, as mentioned earlier. Of course, some would say these are a response to the bad state of our world, although the blatant doomsdaying and subscription to fear on every front by media would also have to account for at least some of this.

The strange thing is we know and accept that boundaries are important in other scenarios. The introductory reality television shows in the early 2000s were often about helping families manage where their children were running amok or obese, or even where pets were causing problems. In each of these scenarios, the answer was providing firm boundaries. This meant providing consequences for unhelpful behaviour and rewarding the required behaviour.

It reminds me of the process we went through when we got a puppy. In many ways, she was quite easy to train. To this day, we can trust her around food and she knows the delineation of where the carpet begins is out of bounds, as well as going outside to relieve herself. Unfortunately, it was a little harder teaching her where home began and ended. As she found every hole in the fence — we have a large property, so this was quite extensive — we found ourselves spending a lot of time patching and repairing the fence and chasing her around the neighbourhood. Unfortunately, she had worked out how to find the weaknesses in the boundary-line and exploit them to gain her freedom. In one sense, we could ask what the problem was with her escaping. She was having a good time and wasn't doing any harm. However, she was not safe and she did cause inconvenience to those who were concerned for her safety when they found her roaming, not to mention the distress it would have caused anyone driving if they hit her while she wandered the streets.

Our laws around cats are another example. Basically, if you want a cat in our area now, you either have to have them completely indoors or have a cat cage. The cat must remain on your property at all times and indoors at night. If you have ever had a cat, you will know the difficulties associated with this. They certainly have their own agendas! However, even though many struggle with this, there are groups of people adamantly wanting to curb and inhibit the freedom of cats to do what comes naturally.

Personally, I am not sure why we think we should treat humans differently to animals, for their own safety and for the safety and comfort of others. It does not seem logical and is not in line with so many other demands our society is now making on behaviour deemed to be bad for the environment, for example. Perhaps it is the selectivity of the freedoms certain groups wish to curtail that is a major part of the issue.

There are many other ways in which we have grown into a society that believes our right to be free trumps that same right in others. As a teacher, students constantly reminded me of their rights when they had impinged on the rights of others and were experiencing the consequences. I continue to see the outworking of this in our communities and society at large.

What should freedom look like?

One of my favourite concepts from the Bible revolves around this issue of freedom. In one of Jesus' first recorded messages, He read from Isaiah 61. Part of that reading talks of bringing freedom to the captives or prisoners. While we might like to interpret this in a physical sense, and indeed, His listeners, as virtual prisoners under harsh Roman rule with a loss of many freedoms most likely did, there is also a spiritual and emotional aspect to this.

What are those things that hold us back, that prevent us from living in freedom, that prevent us from being who God has created us to be? And what do we believe about this?

One problem with our measures of freedom is that we like to think that freedom means that I can do as I please. This is a fallacy because generally when I simply do as I please or simply follow my feelings or desires with no reference to consequences for any length of time, I will eventually get to a place where I can no longer do as I please. I will either have run out of money, run out of supporters, or otherwise entered into circumstances which rob me of any freedom, whether that be drug addiction, jail or loss of income, home, friends and family. An abuse of freedom will inevitably lead to a loss of freedom.

When I was a teen, we had a poster with a picture of the Bible and the words: *"When all else fails, read the manufacturer's instructions"*. Of course, many of us are aware of the flippant observations that men don't like to follow instructions, whether that be in putting something together or directions to a location. There are some hilarious quotes that illustrate this so well. Tim Allen tells us, *"Real men don't use instructions, son. Besides, this is just the manufacturer's opinion on how to put this together*". An anonymous quip takes it another step further, saying,"*Men say women should come with instructions. What's the point? Have you ever seen a man actually read the instructions?*". However, in all our proclivity to doing things our own way, it often doesn't work out the way we hope — especially if it came from IKEA[1]!

Working out the balance between freedom and responsibility is far from straight forward. What is acceptable for one is unhelpful for another. I would suggest it takes a great deal of wisdom greater than our own to properly grasp an manage our freedom well.

---

[1] This is not a negative comment about IKEA, but an observation that the way their products go together are often different to what we expect. If we don't read the instructions first, but decide we know better, at best we may find ourselves doing a "do-over", if not destroying the product.

Exploring equality, inequality and the state of our world

Over time, many have sought the ideal world where everyone gets a fair go and a fair share of the wealth of our planet. However, we seem to move further and further from that ideal, even though, in so many ways, our world is growing smaller. According to some statistics, in 2018 a mere one percent of the global population owned forty-five percent of the world's wealth. The top forty-two most wealthy people own as much as fifty percent of the world's poorest.[19] Others have suggested that royalty from a century or so back in time would envy the way most of us live today in the west. The things we consider basic necessities — hot and cold running water, flushing indoor toilets, refrigeration and the volume and variety of food and clothing afforded us by technology, not to mention all the other non-essential technology we take for granted — were unheard of, let alone imagined not so long ago.

Of course, proponents of socialism and communism hold on to the premise that equality is possible, that everyone should get an equal share of global wealth. While this sounds good in theory, the problem of human greed is a glaring issue in the failure of these ideologies. Rarely are people content to receive the same payment as someone they perceive as not working as hard or without the same skill as themselves. The difficulty is the patently obvious fact that we are not all uniform in our abilities, personalities, wiring and even needs. There really is no such thing as one size fits all when it comes to lifestyle, desires and what we want to do with our lives. Books such as Orwell's *Nineteen Eighty-Four* and *Animal Farm* draw the picture all too clearly of what happens when we try. Perhaps the biggest issue is one of control: those at the top believe they know best and if they can control those below them, they can make it all fair. Unfortunately, this arrogance often fails to recognise the gifts and abilities many nameless and faceless ones bring to our society which could make it better. Control would seem to lead to a lack of performance and initiative in those being controlled. And getting rid of unwanted control and dominance through control and dominance would seem quite counterproductive.

Many in business believe that in order to make money, you have to drive everyone else down to the lowest possible figure — business is purely concerned with the highest profit margins; it is all about making money for the shareholders. The people down the line are irrelevant. An example of this is in the retail industry where those on-selling goods often make 80% or more of the profits while those actually doing the work producing and making the goods generally receive well less than 1% of the final price. The truth is that there is enough margin in these goods for everyone to have a reasonable income, but greed and our desire for more (goods and wealth, particularly without needing to work for it) means we allow and accept this gross inequality.

Although there is a growing awareness of this issue, too often the retailers control the choices of the consumer, limiting their ability to make change. An example in Australia is in our dairy industry, where supermarkets were selling milk at a very low price of around a dollar a litre. While wages and the cost of living has gone up considerably, this is something (along with many other goods) that has actually gone down in price. When I was a teen some thirty plus years ago, my mother put a limit on us of a glass of milk a day because of the expense. I am one of five, so we could easily get through a couple of litres a day. She also used to mix the milk half with powdered milk to make it go further. One site I looked at suggested the equivalent price today would be $2.78/litre.[20] It is the same with clothing, shoes, toys and electrical goods. They are generally so much cheaper, dollar for dollar, than they were thirty or more years ago and yet our wages have continued to increase, not to mention that in many families, both parents work. Added to this is the fact that so much of our manufacturing is now done in countries where wages, expectations and regulations are much lower.

Going back to the milk example, though, it is very difficult as a consumer to make a change. We can buy branded milk instead of supermarket brands, but there is still no guarantee in many cases that the producer — the farmer — will get any more money. Giving more money to the supermarket or department store does not mean they pass on that increased margin to those down the line. This has become so systemic in how economics work in our society and beyond that it will take major upheaval (or a very long, slow process) to make any real change. The reality is that most of us do not care enough to make enough noise about it. And of course, if we vote with our feet and stop purchasing completely, we leave those down line with no income at all.

The good news is that at the micro level, there are people working in some of the countries manufacturering many of our goods to set up businesses that do operate much more fairly, making sure people are paid enough so that their families are provided for and children can have an education. Some factories in these places even supply health and child care to their workers. There is a growing awareness and support of the fair trade concept, which is actually making some difference.

It does make me wonder why we can get so upset about seemingly minor inequalities occurring to us, while we can so easily ignore the huge inequalities between us and those in less developed/industrialised countries. Our perception of our lack so consumes us, while many others don't even have a grid for what we think we lack — they are the idea of luxury to so many. We are terribly affronted because we don't get the opportunities we think we deserve or should have and start calling them human rights, while others don't even have basic access to water, food, sanitation, health care, shelter or safety. We are disinterested and disaffected. Even as we continue to talk about tolerance and inclusion, it appears there is ever greater division, anger and hatred over smaller and smaller differences of ideals. While I agree wholeheartedly that we do need to take care of those who are the most vulnerable in our society, if this is at the expense of everyone else, we need to question whether our methodology is actually helpful.

Exploring sin and its origin

As mentioned earlier, the foundations of our beliefs are fundamentally important to how we live out those beliefs. In truth, we will live out of the foundations rather than what we have built on them. If our foundations are faulty, then the whole house may come crashing down. The question I believe every person, Christian or not, needs to address at some point is what those foundations are. Far too often, I believe that even as Christians with very firmly stated beliefs, we have actually taken our position from the world's perspective and added God on top. We have created Him in our own image, or otherwise distorted Him to fit into the places where we struggle with what the Bible tells us about Him.

Those who seriously study the Bible or any other ancient literature, will understand the importance of context and awareness of cultural differences. In a time when many seem to be assessing so much of the past through then lens of current beliefs and perception, so much can be lost. Comprehension of culture and context are vitally important in helping with many of the difficulties we have understanding God and reconciling some of the more uncomfortable images and stories from the Bible. One that springs to mind is the movement around the idea that Jesus was maybe homosexual because of the relationship He had with His disciples. Anyone who has spent any time around Middle Eastern men can easily debunk this idea. The relationship the average Middle Eastern red-blooded male has with his peers is very physical — they will often sit with arms around each other's shoulders, hug and kiss each other in greeting and there is nothing sexual about it at all. This is a great example of the care we need to take in not overlaying our own societal norms on cultures that are very different from our own, let alone separated by 2000 years or more.

Returning to our foundations, as someone who grew up in a Christian family with generations of Christians, including pastors and missionaries on both sides, I still went through a quite painful process of feeling God digging up my foundations where they were faulty and replacing them with His. While it wasn't every aspect of my foundations, there have been many beliefs I grew up with, both about myself and about the world around me that were less than helpful. Until I dealt with the roots of where they came from, though, they were impacting my life, causing cracks and inconsistencies.

In terms of what we generally believe — accepted truths — as Christians, one of the sticking points for many is the whole starting point of the idea of Original Sin. Growing up in the 1970s, I do remember grappling a little with the idea that was still quite strong in many Christian communities that this was to do with nakedness and hence sexuality. This is still a stronghold in some communities. When we look closely into the account of "the fall" in Genesis 3, though, a number of things have become very plain to me.

The first, in dealing with nakedness and our sexuality, is that God created us naked, for companionship between male and female and (dare I say it!) to procreate. And He said it was good. Who are we to contradict Him? The way my understanding of this has developed is that the problem of our nakedness only occurred in the place of brokenness after sin entered in. I don't think it was ever a problem for God. In terms of our relationship with God, our nakedness embodies our vulnerability or openness to Him. It can be uncomfortable and awkward. We feel exposed when we come before Him because deep down we know we can hide nothing, none of our brokenness and sinfulness from Him.

We can feel the same with others. Our nakedness exposes our weakness and brokenness. Fear has a grip in this place as well as in our place before God. And so, just as Adam and Eve did, we hide from each other and God. We cover up, whether through our clothing (got to love loose clothing for covering up that bit of extra weight!), make up, hair pieces and toupees, position and title, wealth or power, or even our overt embracing of the opposite. We use all these things and more to make ourselves feel less vulnerable. And so, we add layer upon layer onto our faulty foundation, creating an unwieldy, imbalanced and fragile edifice that may or may not topple at anything above the lightest of breezes. Realising this, we add buttresses and scaffolds through more wealth, more money, more grandiose ideas and posturing, but at some point, God will allow an earthquake, a flood, a calamity of some sort — even COVID-19 — to shake and expose where those foundations are faulty or unable to support the beliefs, attitudes and behaviours we have added on top.

The bottom line is that our sin is not found in our nakedness, but in how we deal with it, how we deal with our exposure and vulnerability.

Our nakedness reveals our brokenness.

In my own grappling with the whole creation/fall story, particularly the perceived holes in taking it literally, there was a point where I had to lay down my own rationality and understanding. Starting from a point of faith and reading from there radically changed how I saw this story. However, regardless of whether you see the story as an allegory or as fact, there is much we can take from it and relate to how we see ourselves in regards to God and the rest of creation. If you cannot accept God as creating the world at any level, there is a point where we may part ways. However, if you can accept God as Creator, then hopefully the rest makes sense. The choice that was presented and subsequent failure of Adam and Eve to make a choice that was helpful to them is one we all make at some point and our own failure is there as well. They give us a picture of who we are, warts and all!

The understanding I have of the Fall then, is *the failure at the point of choice to make a good decision*, and it has several layers. The first is listening to a voice other than God's voice particularly when that voice was in opposition. Yes, it was cunningly slight, just *left of centre* so to speak. It wasn't an out and out lie, more a mistruth, a bending and twisting of what has been said: "Did God really say you must not eat from any tree in the garden?" And just as subtly, Eve's response twists God's words from eat to touch (vs 3), "You must not eat fruit from the tree that is in the middle of the garden, and you must not touch it, or you will die". To which the serpent twists a little further and tells her she won't die but be like God, knowing good from evil. There is just enough truth in this, and too much missing, especially the thin line between spiritual and physical death.

The devastating effects of the loss of innocence and living with not just one choice of obedience but a myriad, compounds the situation. Instead of there being only one thing to choose not to do, we are left with layer upon layer of choices between good and evil. In fact, our whole lives and way of being were given over to a different set of foundations. Rather than the basis of living being relationship with God and having Him as our source of all life, we are left working through those countless and constant, incessant, tiring, exhausting, draining choices between good and evil.

And so, as the story continues, Eve chose to listen to what the serpent said, to walk a little down the path and blatantly disobey the one command her Maker had given her. She failed in the one choice and it had devastating consequences. Through the generations since many, including, it would appear, Paul,[21] have blamed Eve for her weakness. Subsequently, in a sense (if not literally), the concept that she is the mother of all sin has lead to all women being tarred with the same brush in some circles. However, we are told in Genesis 3 that Adam was right with her at the time. We cannot absolve him. He failed in his role as protector and as her partner in one flesh. As John Eldredge points out in *Wild at Heart*,

> *"Where is Adam, while the serpent is tempting Eve? He's standing right there...The Hebrew for "with her" means right there, elbow to elbow. Adam*

> *isn't away in another part of the forest; he has no alibi. He is standing right there, watching the whole thing unravel. What does he do? Nothing. Absolutely nothing."*[22]

So inasmuch as Eve was literally the one who disobeyed, Adam was a willing partner. His silence, (and partaking in the fruit), was his consent. He partnered with Eve in the resultant action and all that followed, and so is an equal partner in sin.

If part one was the act of disobedience, the subsequent events sealed the deal and brought the conclusion we have lived with since.

The next mistake they made was to hide. There was no owning up to the mistake. There was no honesty or openness at all. Adam and Eve hid from God. They knew He'd be out walking in the Garden in the evening, and they didn't want to meet up with Him. Not today. So they hid. First they made themselves fig leaf outfits to hide their nakedness, which had become synonymous with their shame, but finding this didn't ease their discomfort they tried whole trees to cover them. And it still didn't work.

We may use God's question, "Where are you?" to belittle God, believing it signifies that God didn't know what was going on, that He was absent from it all. However, parents will know that this is actually a disciplinary strategy in a relationship. It is providing a final opportunity for the perpetrator to come clean. I have often wondered how things may have turned out differently if Adam and Eve had 'fessed up quickly, had gone to God and said how sorry they were and asked forgiveness, asked how they could make up for their disobedience. But they didn't. When questioned, they quickly moved onto the next depth of their sin. Blame. Not taking responsibility for their actions. Adam blames

Eve and God ("the woman You gave me"). Eve blames the devil. And we have been doing it ever since. Not my fault.

We see this pattern in our society and in us as individuals. She/he made me do it. The devil made me do it. And we hide in our shame and refuse to have relationship with those we have hurt including God. Or we at least hide away the bits of us we are ashamed of, whether that be our physical bodies or our past and don't let others into the place of our vulnerability.

This is what I would see as original sin or the origin of sin. Whether we see it as the pattern we learned from Adam and Eve or that Adam and Eve are a picture of the pattern we see played out across the history of humanity and our own lives is largely irrelevant. The far more important question is what we do about it and how we, individually, respond to it. Will we continue to hide? Will we continue to blame everything and everyone else we can think of? Or will we step out from behind these lies and excuses and step up, make ourselves vulnerable, open up and take responsibility?

Are we prepared to be real?

Of course, accepting these problems leads to another problem: our inability to fix what has been broken. As described throughout much of this book, all our efforts thus far have just shown the flaws in our methodology and foundations which, far from improving our global lot only exacerbate the issue, whether we look at it from a physical, emotional or spiritual perspective.

However, the concept of original sin as described here illustrates the foundation on which we have so often built on. It is what Adam and Eve's eyes were opened to that we have never been able to shut. Indeed, it is a tension and struggle we have even as Christians.

> *Our eyes, having been opened to the knowledge of good and evil, have made this the foundation to our lives.*

We have built our lives around the concept that some things are good and some are bad, and in everything, we now have to make this choice. Which is it? We do it over our own lives and ourselves and we do it over the lives of everyone else. Good or bad? Judgement and subsequent condemnation. (For a really helpful investigation of this and how it plays out in our lives, check out *There Were Two Trees in the Garden*, by Rick Joyner.[23])

We have built and developed a way of living on this foundation of fear: fear of doing wrong, fear of making mistakes, fear of hurt and pain, fear of judgement, fear of exposure and ultimately, fear of each other and God. Instead of confidence in the goodness of God, we live from a position of trying to make ourselves good enough that God (and even others) won't smite us.

We work ever harder to be good enough to escape the punishment of death, never quite realising that we are already inhabiting the "living death" of using work to justify our existence, give us purpose and meaning and finding that it is never quite sufficient.

It never quite scratches the itch to make us good enough.

In our current society, we can see this in our obsession with risk assessment. Just as any business or organisation worth their salt will want to understand their exposure to risk, we work to balance acceptable risk with the issue of doing nothing as the ultimate risk protection. The better we believe we can manage our risk exposure, the safer we feel.

A more recent observation is that we have moved to a position of making our safety (or at least, sense of safety) our god, the most important aspect of life. In many Western cultures, we have moved another step forward, relegating our safety to our governments, handing them the responsibility to not only tell us how to stay safe, but with enforcing laws to prevent people making their own choices. Far from becoming autonomous adults who take responsibility for the consequences of our actions, we are still looking for someone else to blame if it doesn't quite work out how we'd like. In the process, we have renounced our freedom, albeit a freedom to make mistakes and to live with the consequences of our actions. And yet, even with all these perceived protectors, there will always be unforeseen risks that sideswipe us while we continue to live in the belief that insurance, whether that is financial or other methods, will protect us, or at least give us the ability to restore anything we have lost.

Living a life based on fears has its own risks. As much we like to think we live fear free or can "feel the fear and do it anyway", if we scratch the surface, most of us will find fear lurking and feeding into at least one aspect of our lives. It might not be behavioural in the traditional sense of heights, people, crowded spaces, spiders, snakes, water, and so on. It could be fear of intimacy, of commitment, of loss or failure, which is exactly what insurance is all about: protection for all we fear might come upon us. We all struggle with fear at some level…unless of course, we have done a great deal of work in that area, but that's another book.

To deal with these foundations requires us to have a significant mental shift, digging up generations of beliefs to find an alternative way of being.

Exploring intellectual assent

Intellectual assent as I understand it, is the act of agreeing with something in theory, but not actually allowing it to impact our behaviour or way of life. An example would be acknowledging statistics that show seat belts to greatly decrease serious injury in an accident, saying I believe that seat belts are important and useful, but never actually wearing a seat belt in the car. It could be closely associated with double-mindedness and hypocrisy. When we agree with something in our mind, but there is no corresponding transformation of our hearts or our behaviours and attitudes, it is very easy to become either hypocritical or we are double-minded in that we are not actually living out what we say we believe.

If we claim to believe one thing, but live according to a different set of beliefs and values that are in conflict with the first set of beliefs we could almost be termed as having a split personality. We might have one persona we let loose when we are around other Christians or like minded individuals, or involved in spiritual activities and an often quite different persona we use for our secular activities. Unfortunately (or fortunately), at some point this will leave us in a place of conflict, either internally or externally, especially if someone catches us out! This concept could explain why some (particularly) in high level Church/Christian leadership positions can have extra-marital affairs, abuse their power and position or embezzle funds and still seem to function as though all is well.

Christianity, however, was always supposed to be controversial, putting its adherents at odds with the world. It is not just a different way of living, but a whole different underlying philosophy, understanding and foundation of what is true. Our calling is not only to live differently, but to respond differently. We fight and war differently, we take ground for the Kingdom of God differently. Jesus calls us to win by laying down our lives. He calls us to fight by loving our enemies, by doing good to them and by blessing them. However, as I have repeatedly proposed, if we continue to build our faith on the same foundations as the world, we can hardly expect a different outcome.

As mentioned earlier, I grew up with the scientific model of thinking all around me. It has been interesting to look back into my family tree and realise that what I thought was simply normal actually wasn't. Something I saw as a non-negotiable (finish secondary school, go to university, work in a profession, all with a huge emphasis on doing pure sciences and mathematics) was not actually the only way to live a valuable life. Even the fact that my father had these expectations of me (as the only daughter in a family of five children) didn't strike me as anything other than a burden until more recently. I came to realise that not many other girls my age had the opportunities or encouragements that I assumed as commonplace — not that I particularly enjoyed being the only girl in my physics class and one of two in chemistry and mathematics classes!

In reflecting on my family history, I grasped the significance of the fact that my great-grandfather had been quite progressive (dare I use that word) and thereby instrumental in opening the way for me. He sent all his daughters to university, the eldest becoming one of the first woman doctors in their city. Another of these daughters was my father's mother. It was very rare back in the early 1900s and this concept of educating women in the sciences was handed down through the generations to become normal in my family line.

More recently, though, I have found myself dealing with this way of thinking afresh. It was difficult enough when my own daughter reached that age, releasing her from the expectations and beliefs so ingrained in me. Even though I had long since realised that I had followed a path that really wasn't my forte, and having gone on and done further study in areas that interested me a great deal more, I still struggled with letting go of the perceived status associated in my mind with these sorts of studies. When I pulled apart my feelings, I could see that these subjects had not really furthered my career prospects, but had simply been a heavy weight.

In fact, there was a point in my life where I needed to break agreement with some of these beliefs which, although they had been helpful in giving me freedom and advancement in the prevalent world view, were holding me back in my relationship with God and in trusting Him. There was an underlying belief there that didn't line up with the rest of what I said I believed. One of the phrases that came to mind was *"knowledge is power"*.

It was difficult to let go of this belief. It is one that has the appearance of truth at so many levels. However, it also put me in the position of believing that I needed to know and understand everything to have power (or control over my life outcomes), but also, that I should or needed to have that power. Even further, it engaged the lie that through knowledge I could control every outcome. This is counter to faith and trust, particularly in God's strength and power rather than my own. It kept me tied (and probably still impacts me to a degree) to the idea that God is not enough, that He needs my help to fix the world or even just my life.

In many ways, beliefs such as these appear helpful because they give us the illusion that they can protect us. We currently live in a world where trust has been broken on so many levels, in so many ways and so many times. Each time our trust is broken, it takes longer and longer to rebuild. We put in more and more layers of protection against having our trust is broken — we come to expect people to be untrustworthy. Added to this, so many aspects of our lives, beliefs and understanding seem to be dictated by what those with a voice deem essential rights and entitlements. The outworking of this is that many people now struggle to trust those in authority. Whether it is because of the exposure of outright lies told by some, or just finding that those who are supposed to represent us and take care of our nation are not always doing what we would like or believe to be right, our confidence in them has been broken. There are aspects where this also impacts our trust in God. When we don't see Him *in control* in the way we would like, do we come to a place where we believe that we can only trust ourselves, only trust in our own strength and ability?

This leads us back to working it all out for ourselves using our own wisdom and perspective. However, a major problem I see with the scientific model of thinking, which is closely aligned in this, is that the emphasis on rationality, logic and fact is quite limiting. The first, most obvious point (to me, anyway) is that what we designate as fact is based on those aspects of the world around us we can quantify: those we can measure and those with some sort of constancy. The problem is, this assumes we already know enough to be able to observe everything necessary.

A great example of this is the bat. Historically, people could not understand how bats functioned in the world as they appeared to have very little vision and unable to make sounds. This made people very fearful of bats and led to many superstitious beliefs regarding them. It wasn't until the 1920s when it was discovered they used frequencies above the range of human hearing to echo locate that there was more understanding. The point here is that our limited understanding can either close our minds to possibilities beyond what we already know, or merely lead us down the proverbial garden path.

When I went back to study psychology in the early 2000s, this was further illustrated to me. Discussion about the methodology of conducting psychological studies and the associated issue of them simply showing up what most people already innately know, exposed the problem with scientific research of all types. In order to have theory and knowledge accepted as reality, and even published, usually it has to either underpin or expand on what others have already established. The only way to present something new and different to previously accepted information is to produce many counter statistics, demonstrated by multiple repeatable experimentation in controlled conditions by validated scientific method. The costs associated with this are rarely forthcoming for anything that might change the status quo. Basically, it means that the only scientific research that generally receives funding and promotion is that which serves the current metanarrative (overarching story/belief) of those in positions of power. We don't want the metanarrative that we (humans) are in control and are beyond accountability (to anyone other than ourselves) to be upset or debunked, so only that which supports that metanarrative attains support and publicity.

Western culture has developed a worldview that still struggles to see beyond these parameters set by previous generations. Just as philosophers and scientists felt they had to break free from the confines of the religious world view of the day back in the 1600s, (although there is evidence those in the middle east and China had been using observation and experimentation for some 400 and more years before this), we are perhaps entering an era where we need to swing the pendulum back a little way to admit that there is plenty we can't observe or put into a neat theory or fact sheet, that we can't put into a neat intellectual box with a clean, provable answer like 2+2=4.

One of our key issues, of course, is about control. We like to know that "if I do x, then y will happen" and be able to accurately predict outcomes. Much of this comes back to our desire to feel safe, or even just to get our own way, even though we learn quite early on as children that this doesn't always work. The point is, when we limit what we know about the world and how it functions simply to science and what we deem rational thinking, we cannot know whether we are actually missing some vital information.

If we came across a piece of equipment that was completely foreign to us and we had no idea about what the owners used it for, we could make many assumptions about its operation. They may or may not be correct and may or may not be successful for us, whether that is what the creator designed it for or not. Unless we had a manual we could read or could speak to someone who knew what the object was created for and how it operated at peak functionality, we may, at best only get limited use from it, and may, at worst, completely destroy it in the process by using it for something for which it was never designed. If we look at planet Earth through this lens, it is obvious we have been doing just this, whether we believe in a Creator or not. (A great and hilarious exposé of this concept is found in the movie, *The God's Must Be Crazy*. A soda bottle is thrown out of an aeroplane and is found by a Kalahari bushman, who has little interaction with the rest of the world. Having no previous experience or parameters to explain what the bottle is, or its purpose, the calamity that ensues leads him to conclude it is an item of great evil, of which he wants no part. Maybe he wasn't so wrong!)

Yet again, this brings us back to the concept of the foundations we build our beliefs on. Our belief (or not) in a Creator God would have to be the most crucial in its impact on all our other beliefs. Unfortunately, many people do not see or understand how incompatible many of their beliefs are. They have a mixed worldview, or perhaps it is simply that the god they think they believe in is vastly different to the story their behaviour would tell.

What I mean by this is that what we believe about a creator god is just as important as whether or not we believe. If we start from the perspective of non-belief, or atheism, the cry I hear from many who espouse this belief is, "I can't believe in a god who would/wouldn't…" My observation of many atheists is that they are actually quite angry with the god they don't believe in.

I wonder if there is not a great deal of hurt, pain and disappointment somewhere in their past, where God did not turn up for them in the way they would have liked or supposedly allowed something to happen that has left them in deep pain. Have they made God responsible for something that perhaps was not His responsibility?

When I read Richard Dawkins' book *The God Delusion*,[24] what struck me most was a paucity of argument against God. In his introduction he declares belief in God as "an evasion of responsibility". He goes on to declare, "it invokes the very thing it is supposed to be explaining" as a reason why the argument is flawed. He then, in turn, invokes the laws of physics as being "fine-tuned in such a way as to set up the conditions…" It leaves me with a big question of who fine-tuned them? Language itself would argue against him. Reading on in the introduction, he further accuses Christians of laziness because of the numbers of people who identify as Christian for every belief except as accepting Jesus as their Lord and Saviour. Unfortunately, we all know that just because we self-identify as something, it doesn't make it true! The concept of what it means to be a Christian can have different connotations depending on who you ask. Seeing the behaviour and attitudes of many Christians online, I know I am not alone in not always wanting to identify with the Christian label these days as it may come with some very unhelpful baggage. (Perhaps we could revert to a follower of Jesus/Yeshua or The Way?)

Much of Dawkins' criticisms of those with faith comes across as very emotive, as well as portraying Christians as something of a caricature of what I would believe a Christian should be like (even though his caricature is probably quite correct in some regards). Added to this, his criticism of faith as being lazy or defeatist when stating that we don't need to understand everything begs the question of what will happen if we don't know or understand every aspect of the world we live in. What is the point or outcome we are looking for by understanding everything? If it is about control or our idea of making things better, what makes us think we have the right better or that our way is right? And this doesn't even begin to deal with the question of whether we can possibly know everything. The idea that our efforts can get us out of the mess our own efforts caused seems quite circular if not lining up with the definition of insanity, where we keep doing the same things and expect different results. In my own journey, I have found a great deal of freedom and rest in trusting God and not having to understand everything.

Again, this leads us back to the idea of human supremacy. It leads us to focussing on our own ability to not only fix things, but also taking responsibility for everything that is wrong. How can we know *what* is right? How do we decide *who* is right? Because if it is me, and not you, this leads us straight back to domination and control of others (a lack of the freedom we so desire). And if we want to say everyone is free to do what they want as long as it doesn't hurt anyone else (and just how do we measure hurt?), we find ourselves in the place of "everyone did as they saw fit" (Judges 17:6), which, as we can imagine, pretty much leads to chaos and destruction, otherwise known as anarchy.

In this place of doing as we see fit, many of us actually turn ourselves into gods, where the god is the one who must be pleased. It is interesting to note that as we have given more and more freedom to successive generations, there is some evidence that suggests the prevalence of narcissism has also risen.[25] Some of the signs of narcissism are: excessive need for admiration (how many *likes* did your last post get?); disregard for others' feelings (cyber bullying anyone?); an inability to handle any criticism and a sense of entitlement (my rights are way more important than my responsibilities).[26]

One concept of a god is that they must be served and kept happy for our lives to be good. A problem that occurs when we allow ourselves or our children to become demi-gods (or greater, which is actually where the term narcissism comes from — the Narcissus was the name of a Greek god) is that those who are the gods are never truly pleased. The more we sacrifice to them and try to appease them, the more they crave. The cycle is truly addictive, where, like all good addicts, they need more and more to have the same effect. These gods don't have a set of regulations that can be known and comprehended, but are capricious and changeable, constantly crying out for greater and greater control and influence. Their way is the only way.

Of course, that is not to say that everything was great and perfect in past history. There were behaviours and rules endorsed or even imposed by the church and Christians that have not been helpful and have been far from what Jesus taught. Greed, corruption, self-serving and control have infiltrated communities of believers, bringing the expected outcomes of brokenness, disunity and eventually destruction.

The answer, according to some, is to outlaw all religions as these are the problem. Without religions, they assert, people would behave much better and we wouldn't have any of the problems we do. As many of our Western nations move away from being Christian, and have less and less people identifying as such, I wonder if we are really seeing the better society we crave? (It is interesting to note, more recently Dawkins has acknowledged that a lack of any belief in God may give "people a licence to do really bad things", and that society might be worse without religion.[27] Perhaps logic and reason can point back to God as well!)

In a society where so many aspects of our education system have been actively renouncing any idea of God and teaching children that our universe is just an accident for some decades now, I believe we have actually removed hope from them. And this is what we see consistently in our society — a culture where the erosion of hope has become widescale. Student marches and protests about climate change illustrate another arena where we have told our children that there is no hope — or that the only way there is any hope of saving our world is to radically change our society in a number of areas. While I agree that we do need to change much of what we do, especially with our consumerist lifestyle and focus on self-comfort and self-indulgence, I am not sure that we can reverse the trajectory we are on by our own efforts. I guess it comes back to whether you believe that we, as humans, are not only responsible to fix our planet but also, that we are capable to do so. (Although, if you believe we are a product of evolution and a random accident, why you would need to take on this responsibility, I am not sure.)

Looking at the last few millennia of our efforts, perhaps some see us as being more advanced than in the past, but then, the trajectory of our advancement or so called progress also seems to be what has caused this mess. While we would like to think we are smarter and doing things differently, most of the time all we have done is change the colour or the style, but the underlying principles and foundations are just the same.

If say we believe in Creator God, if we say believe in His sovereignty, and that He is who the Bible portrays Him to be, then there is a point at which we really need to dig deep into what we give agreement to in terms of what is propagated as truth around how the world operates. We can not afford to pick bits and pieces that we like and stick them together as a whole "truth" and live our lives out of this space. A word I have been exploring more deeply of late is the Hebrew word we translate as peace — Shalom. Far from just an absence of war or disquiet, it also encompasses concepts of wholeness and integrity (consistency of behaviour reflecting stated beliefs), for starters. When we pick up the parts of Christianity that work for us and add them to pieces of beliefs from other aspects of the world, we end up with incongruence, which is far from the shalom peace promised by Jesus. We must move out of the place of our behaviour mismatching our stated beliefs, but we cannot do it alone.

Exploring righteousness and justification

Righteousness and justification are two words that can have quite negative connotations. In Christian circles they have often become *Christian-ese* that gets bandied about with little to no understanding or meaning. On the flip side, in society at large, attitudes and behaviours promoting self-righteousness and self-justification are seen as very unattractive qualities. However, like many terms that seem to have lost or been reassigned meaning, these two need to be rediscovered. Underneath our apparent lack of care or awareness around these concepts, I doubt many of us enjoy being seen as either evil or unjust in our actions. The amount of time spent on social media trying to prove that we are both good and justified give support to this.

Obviously, no one enjoys being wrong or even in the wrong. In fact, I would suggest that most, if not all fights and wars result from the battle over who is right and who is wrong. Whether it be in regards to land ownership, religion, or more mundane issues such as a difference of opinion, if someone crosses our particular line, we come out swinging, either physically or metaphorically. And sometimes, even when we know we are in the wrong, our sense of honour, self-protection or simple pride leads us to a point where we will still fight over it rather than deal more constructively with our feelings of humiliation or humble ourselves enough to say sorry. Our drive to be right so often supplants our desire for relationship and so we use accusations and blame to shift the focus from our own behaviour onto someone else.

As mentioned earlier, right back at the beginning of the Bible we see the model of behaviour that is now rife in our world, where we blame each other, blame the devil or blame God when we find ourselves on the wrong side.

Although, as a society we generally don't like these labels, the opposite of being in the wrong may be termed either being righteous or justified. Unfortunately, this often manifests itself as being self-righteous or punitive — you hurt me somehow, so that justifies me paying you back. It is only fair. We use this language to vindicate our actions when we perceive that someone else has done the wrong thing by us, or when we think we have the upper hand morally.

In addition, we use our judgement to either stroke or condemn others. To those we deem *on our side*, or whom we would like to be *on our side*, we assert how much they deserve whatever good may come their way. Check on social media how often you read statements like, "good on you, you deserve it". To those we judge not so great, we are just as likely to proclaim deserving of any bad that they experience. We call it karma and self-righteously celebrate our own sense that justice has been done.

Today, the boundaries of what was morally acceptable in the past have shifted immensely from where they were a few short decades ago. From same sex marriage to abortion, to veganism, the pendulum seems to have swung from one extreme to the other. From a position where the complaint was that society should not have the right to determine people's behaviour in these areas, we have now shifted to telling people they are not allowed to have the old opinion; that their opinion must come into line with the official policy of those with the loudest voice. This has been labelled *progressive* thinking. It is others who determine the correct moral decision for us with no room for discussion. Far from having choice, others tell us what we must believe; how we must think; what we must do, or we will find ourselves on the wrong side of history, on the wrong side of morality and on the wrong side of society. It is so prevalent, we even have a name for it: virtue signalling. "Look how good I am because I follow all the progressive mandates."

The major, largely unanswered question here is who gets to decide what is right or wrong? As a culture, what is the measure or guide that we are using? When we throw out past measures of what was unacceptable or not deemed progressive, what bench mark do we now use? It would appear that we change laws and change what we judge appropriate, and give it the label "progressive", giving the message it is better than what was before, that previous laws are now outdated and those who want to fit in and be acceptable had better conform.

It reminds me very much of the old fable of *The Emperor's New Clothes* by Hans Christian Andersen. In the story, two clever weavers (or con men) come to town to make a vain emperor a new set of clothing. They convince everyone that their fabric is so special that anyone who is stupid or unfit for their job won't be able to see it. Of course, when the emperor finally comes to try the clothes on, no one can see anything but his underwear, but not wanting to appear stupid or lose their jobs or lives, they all say how magnificent these clothes are. It takes a child to point out the obvious. I often feel we live in a time where many are saying exactly this: if you don't believe this, think that or agree with the other, then you are stupid or deficient in some way. Conform and agree or be ostracised or worse.

Interestingly, we are defining a new morality and perception of righteousness that seems to have no roots or underpinnings other than an opinion or a particular interpretation of data, or even just making certain groups within society feel good about themselves. It seems very much based on what is *flavour of the month*. Although we may dress it up in the ideology of freedom of expression or freedom of behaviour, it would actually appear to achieve the opposite. Just as in George Orwell's *Animal Farm*,[28] by trying to overthrow past tyrants have we only replaced them with further tyrants, who are perhaps worse than those they replaced? While we want to get rid of those we see as repressing us, unless we have a well thought out, tried and tested new regime, then what surety do we have of something better?

Returning to the Garden of Eden and the tree of the knowledge of good and evil, we so often make our determination according to what we see as *good*, or *better* as opposed to what is *bad* or *not so good*. We live out of a belief system that tells us these are the only two choices we have: either something is *good* or it is *evil*. When these are our parameters, it sets us up with a judgement system that seems nice and simple. With enough wisdom and enough facts, it should be quite straightforward to determine right from wrong, good from bad.

But what if we are actually asking the wrong question?

Exploring good, evil and life

Part of our problem is that we like things to be on a linear scale. I remember years ago hearing a speaker ask about the *sin* scale. For example, if Hitler was on the totally depraved and evil end of the scale and Mother Theresa was on the saintly end, where would you place yourself? The explanation is that there is no scale.

As much as we would like it to be otherwise, we don't get *in* or *out* of heaven or even relationship with God by our measure of goodness or badness. Even our blessings and God's favour are not a measure. Jesus makes it quite plain in His teaching found in Matthew 5:45 that God's blessings are given to all. Nevertheless, we tend to live and act as though we believe if we try hard enough and work more and more towards being good it should be enough, or should get us more blessings, more acceptance or more favour than those who are not so good.

However, there are no behaviours within ourselves that can reverse or extricate us from the effects of our brokenness. While I know there are some out there who would like to believe that we are born without the tendency toward sin (bad behaviour), we still have to ask where we learn our bad behaviour from. The response a friend gave me to this question was that *bad parenting* was the issue. However, when I asked where these parents learnt their bad parenting, there was no further answer. Even to say "bad parenting" is a judgement that tells me I can do better and actually raise perfect children, or at least "good enough" children. Again, though, what is the measure of what good enough even looks like? If we recognise any brokenness in people or our society, there must be a starting point to where it all began. Something must have triggered it.

As I researched for this book, an interesting perspective that came across my path was the difference between the Greek worldview as opposed to the Hebraic worldview. It is not something we generally recognise in our society simply because the Greek worldview is so prevalent it has actually become synonymous with the Western worldview. In fact, it is so pervasive that we don't even comprehend that there could be another way of thinking or living.

If we look back in history to the time of the Greek philosophers, as previously mentioned, their main focus for understanding the world was through fact, logic and reason, very much based in the physical realm, with little interest past anything that wasn't measurable. In our Western mode of thinking, we have made this the foundation of our way of living and determining truth or reality. Even if we do, perchance, become aware of the shortfall and the lack of correspondence with many of our supposed ideals, without an alternative, we keep building onto this foundation. Equally, numbers of us just like to keep our head in the sand, hoping if we ignore it, it will all go away. We haven't stopped to reassess our direction, but simply keep adding more on to the top – an adjustment here, a tuck there, without realising that if the foundations are not good, the building will eventually collapse.

In contrast, the traditional Hebraic way of thinking is far more relational. Far from being clean cut and orderly or predictable, it does carry peace, freedom and rest in allowing life to unfold as it will. When we stop trying to control every outcome way past our actual ability to control, we can let go of responsibility for that which is clearly not our responsibility. Rather than putting everything into neat blocks of where we think they fit, the lines blur. Reconciled relationships with God, with each other and with the world around us are the pivot around which all life operates.

Some further details of differences between the Greek mindset and the Hebrew mindset, according to Torah Life Ministry, [29] include the western tendency to segregate or compartmentalise the various aspects of life, whereas the Hebrew mindset sees everything as overlapping or interconnected. This is something our medical model is fast realising the truth of, especially in terms of the links between physical and mental health and whole of life wellness, as an example.

Another distinction is the individualism and desire to not be accountable to others of the Greek/Western mindset, as opposed to the concept of valuing our relationships with every aspect of our world and being accountable — ultimately to God — for all of it. Social life in the Hebrew world view is far more important than simple biological life, which comes back to relationship over functionality again. (Slighty off topic, but quite relevent, there is a very interesting discussion around emotions, physical health and community outcomes between Russell Brand and Lisa Feldman Barrett (Professor of Neuroscience). In extensive studies, Feldman Barrett and others reinforce the idea that our indiviualistic society does not benefit anyone. The idea that poverty actually costs society far more than ensuring no one lives in poverty is particularly interesting in light of the Gospel message. While I don't necessarily agree with all their beliefs and ideas, much of it supports what I have been observing around the issues with how our world is trying to function and the changes that need to happen for improvement in outcomes.[30])

In Genesis 2:9, two trees are mentioned. The difference between these two trees — the tree of life and the tree of the knowledge of good and evil — give us insight into two distinct ways of living. If we are operating from the position of the knowledge of good and evil, the questions we continually ask are: "Is it good? Am I good? Are you good?" None of the answers to these questions bring true freedom or life, but all lead to death, because at some point, the answer is invariably "no". And then, eventually we also come up against the fact that our measure of what is good can be extremely subjective. All this model of living provides us with is a bright, shining light showing up our failings and brokenness.

However, the concept of the tree of life gives us a different question. Does this produce life? In me? In you? In our world? Much of the time, these are not questions that we can necessarily answer by ourselves, although many of us have probably been aware of times when we have felt discomforted by something said or done. There can be a sense that it looks or sounds *good*, but deep inside, we are ill at ease – something is not quite right.

An example for me has come from a number of messages I have listened to in numerous church services. It all sounds ok, sounds like it is from the Bible, there is Scripture used to back it up, but there is a disconnect, something isn't sitting quite right. When I came across the different question, "Does it lead to life or death?" I suddenly realised what the problem was. So much of our teaching is based on the perception that the way forward is about *doing* something to make ourselves right or better; about self-improvement. Whether it is serving, giving or even worshipping — if we do it as a measure of our righteousness and goodness, or acceptability, even to God, we have now fallen back into consuming from the wrong tree. The main problem with this is that what is "good or bad" for me, might be life-giving to you, at least in some cases. Sometimes we have to work this out as we go.

Anytime our behaviour or actions become about "do this and you will get this result", we have fallen into the trap of believing that we have the ability to make ourselves acceptable, or, that getting the outcome we want is based in legalism and rules. Underlying this is the concept of *wishful* or *magical* thinking, which is about manipulating and controlling God/gods, or making ourselves god. This is what idolatry and witchcraft is really about.

> "Jesus didn't come to make *bad* men *good*, but to make **DEAD** men **LIVE**"
>
> - LEONARD RAVENHILL

Exploring law and religion

All too often, we have used the concept of God's Law as a stick to beat people up with, without really understanding what that law is about. Lauritia Hayes[31] points out that if we believe obeying law is just about pleasing a *capricious god*, a god who might change his mind at a whim, that his law has no basis in any truth or foundation then we will continue to see it as an imposition. Like children with parents who only intermittently punish certain behaviours, we live in fear and uncertainty, or eventually, rebellion and anger.

If, instead we see law as being about how our universe operates, just like the laws of physics, which include elements such as gravity and the speed of light, then we realise that *far from being punitive, they become life giving*. Just as we teach our children not to play on the freeway because we love them and don't want to see them hurt or killed, the Law of God is about boundaries and regulations that not only help us to live well, but every other living creature on our planet also.

However, the truth becomes skewed when we forget the underlying foundation of God's Law. If we understood properly that God's Law comes out of His love, and indeed, love is not only the foundation but the essence and building blocks of law, we may respond differently. As Paul points out in Romans 13:8-10:

> *"Owe no one anything, except to love each other, for the one who loves another has fulfilled the law. For the commandments, "You shall not commit adultery, You shall not murder, You shall not steal, You shall not covet," and any other commandment, are summed up in this word: "You shall love your neighbour as yourself." Love does no wrong to a neighbour; therefore love is the fulfilling of the law."*

In the end, we each must make a choice for ourselves.

The story of Moses meeting with God on Mount Sinai in Exodus 19-20 has long illustrated for me the way many of us want to live. For many of the Israelites, just like Adam and Eve after their unhelpful choices, being face to face, vulnerable and open with God was all too scary. Somewhere along the road, they had picked up the idea that God was indeed capricious, or at the very least, quite dangerous. Instead of connecting with Him and finding out the truth of how to have relationship with Him, they preferred someone else to intercede on their behalf. So they requested that Moses go and find out what they should do so God wouldn't smite them.

Many of us would still like to operate the same way: just give me the rules so I can get on with life how I like, walking as close to the line as possible without crossing it. Or maybe even working out how I can bend that line to suit my desires. Or perhaps just wanting to know that I am *good* (enough).

This is one of the major problems with simply putting Christianity in a box as a religion. We turn it into being about rules and regulations, rather than about relationship. There is a choice we need to make and which ever way we choose, we must apply the same measure to every other person on the planet if we are to have integrity and wholeness.

༄

Do we want to live using laws, rules and regulations to give us our acceptability, our "goodness", or do we want to live in freedom through the law of love?

༄

And if we choose relationship, we must then decide to whom we give the ultimate governance in that relationship.

༄

> *Will we try to be judge, jury and executioner ourselves, as our protection mechanism, or are we prepared to lay down our control (and manipulation) and allow God to reign and rule via His life-giving love?*

༄

Perhaps this choice leaves you with more questions than answers, but in my view, that is what the journey of life with our Creator is all about. As we journey with Him, experiencing His grace, peace, mercy, joy, goodness, love, all else tends to fade into insignificance and we just want more of Him.

"You will seek me and find me when you seek me with all your heart."

(Jeremiah 29:13)

In the end...

When I started to write this book, two passages of scripture from Isaiah came to mind, which I will come to shortly. To me, they sum up much of what this book is about. The first is getting our perspective right. As much as we would like to get everything neatly tied up so that we can have certainty around outcomes; certainty, and ultimately control about our destinies, there is no doubt that we never will have that certainty. This includes God. The very nature of God, in any form is a being who is beyond our complete comprehension as well as our control. Any other way, and we become god instead.

The other aspect is that from God's perspective, most of our world looks very different to how we think it is. His laws and the way things work in His Kingdom are often the opposite of how we see them from our viewpoint. I am reminded again and again of just how radical Jesus Christ — Yeshua Messiah — was to every aspect of the era He first turned up in. I don't believe His Way is any less radical today.

As the world steps into another new era, it is very clear to me that so often what we think is the issue is not the issue at all. My thoughts around this have been brewing for the last couple of years. However, in the months of 2020 and into 2021, as we have all been scrambling to find a way, a grid, with which to gain some understanding or at least a foothold as our world has shifted so dramatically, a myriad of answers have been proposed. I have observed a desperate desire to know the *truth* about what is going on, many of us trying to find what we see as a measure of safety and even a perception of control in the *knowing*. Simultaneously, it has become increasingly difficult to really know what is fact and what is fiction.

In the middle of all this change and concern, I have come to the conclusion that it is not so much about a virus, vaccines and big pharma or one world government; it is not about what is conspiracy theory or not; or even what has truly gone on with various elections, to name a few. If I could label a major aim of the enemy of our souls, it would be division. This, I believe is the greatest threat to our world: to create maximum division, leading to hatred, bitterness and ultimately, as many lives and relationships destroyed through this as possible. In this division between right and left, right and wrong, "woke" and asleep, I keep seeing God come in with His ways, His answers, from a totally different direction. Not only does He *not* align with any of the factions, but His way can only be seen and understood as we lay down all that we humanly believe we know and understand. We have to start afresh as little children, seeing through the eyes of spirit, not flesh. Continuing to do the same things and expecting different results is the proverbial lunacy. Why do we keep doing it?

Linking this back to the passages from Isaiah I mentioned earlier, the first is Isaiah 29:13-16. It speaks of an assault on those who think they can tell God what is what, who think that human reasoning will give us all the answers we need.

> *"These people come near to me with their mouth*
> *and honour me with their lips,*
> *but their hearts are far from me.*
> *Their worship of me*
> *is based on merely human rules they have been taught.*
> *Therefore once more I will astound these people*
> *with wonder upon wonder;*
> *the wisdom of the wise will perish,*
> *the intelligence of the intelligent will vanish."*
> *Woe to those who go to great depths*
> *to hide their plans from the Lord,*
> *who do their work in darkness and think,*
> *"Who sees us? Who will know?"*
> *You turn things upside down,*
> *as if the potter were thought to be like the clay!*
> *Shall what is formed say to the one who formed it,*
> *"You did not make me"?*
> *Can the pot say to the potter,*
> *"You know nothing"?*

Interestingly, rather than God coming and turning things upside down, He tells us that we are the ones who have done so. There is also a promise that He will show us a different way of being, taking us back to the right relationships we were created to have.

In Isaiah 55:1-3, 6-9 there is further description of the radical difference of the ways of the Kingdom of God compared to human, or the world's way.

> *"Come, all you who are thirsty,*
> *come to the waters;*
> *and you who have no money,*
> *come, buy and eat!*
> *Come, buy wine and milk*
> *without money and without cost.*
> *Why spend money on what is not bread,*
> *and your labour on what does not satisfy?*
> *Listen, listen to me, and eat what is good,*
> *and you will delight in the richest of fare.*
> *Give ear and come to me;*
> *listen, that you may live…*
> *Seek the LORD while he may be found;*
> *call on him while he is near.*
> *Let the wicked forsake their ways*
> *and the unrighteous their thoughts.*
> *Let them turn to the LORD, and he will have mercy on them,*
> *and to our God, for he will freely pardon.*
> *"For my thoughts are not your thoughts,*
> *neither are your ways my ways,"*
> *declares the LORD.*
> *"As the heavens are higher than the earth,*
> *so are my ways higher than your ways*
> *and my thoughts than your thoughts.""*

Both of these passages highlight the differences between our way of thinking and God's, or, dare I say it, the Truth. They point to perhaps one of the most confronting truths of all, that we are not God, and that no matter how hard we try, or how much we wish it were otherwise, we will always be lower than Him. We don't get to tell Him what is what or even how we would like it to be. This is the first step in getting our relationship with

Him right. A few words that haven't had much traction in most Christian circles in the last few decades perhaps need some re-examination: *submitting, surrendering* and *sacrificing* to God and His authority in our lives and learning the what the *fear of the Lord* actually means.

Once we realise that our life only has meaning and purpose in connection with Him, and with Him as the starting point, or Source of all we need, we are closer to being ready to relate to the rest of the world. More and more, I am personally realising the importance of God as our Source. It is only as I receive His unconditional love that I can step into relationship with Him — when I stop trying to make myself good enough or acceptable to Him first. According to 1 John 4:8, this is the same as receiving Him, because He is love; love is the very essence of His nature. I can only truly love others and truly partake in what it means to be part of the Kingdom of God as much I receive His love. It is as I accept His unconditional love for me that I can accept myself in all my imperfection and at the same time desire to be more like Him. From this point I can begin to do the same for others.

A major impact I observe of the Church trying to compete with the Greek way of thinking, through rationality and logic, is the loss of encounter and experience with God through real relationship. In many ways, we have tried to turn our faith into intellectual or cerebral knowledge, something people can give *intellectual assent* to: An idea that they agree is valid or worthy of contemplation, or even aspiration. However, while many have agreed with the tenets of Christianity, there has been a distinct lack in those experiences with God that lead to transformation. I recently heard the tragic story of a pastor who was dying and asked the nurse caring for him, "Is God real?" At the point of death, this man came to the realisation that while he knew a lot about God, he hadn't actually encountered God. We have replaced encounter and experience with behaviour modification and another set of rules, using motivational speakers and activities to try to help people reach the bar we have set for what we propose is Christian behaviour. This has turned Christianity into just another religion instead of the relationships it is actually about.

Years ago I read a statement in a book by Daniel Kolenda that resonated deeply with me, to the point I use it often (unfortunately, I can't remember the book it was in, so my apologies if it is not word perfect!) :

"Too often we give people an explanation that is in need of an experience. What would happen if they had an experience in need of an explanation?"

If our relationship with God has no power to change us, if we have not and are not being transformed from "glory into glory" (2 Corinthians 3:18), then we will find ourselves back on that hamster wheel, continually trying to fix ourselves, make ourselves more acceptable and worthy, both to God and each other. There is a better way.

In the meantime, we must return to the issue of division and disunity. Many of us grapple with that hard choice between standing on what we see as immutable truth and preserving relationships. We believe we cannot have a relationship with people with whom we disagree. This is not truth. Finding a way to keep relationship in the middle of conflict in a healthy way is not always straightforward and processes are rarely the answer. I do believe an important element, however, is our confidence in who we are in our relationship with God, as individuals, but also seeing others through the same lens. When we are no longer trying to get our identity or love needs from what we perceive from others, we become continually freer to not only accept others as they are in the place of disagreement, but to truly love them. This is where I believe the Kingdom of God can not only reside, but thrive and grow. We get to be part of it.

The choice is yours.

APPENDIX

1   See page 31

2   An influencer in social media is someone who has "built a reputation for their knowledge and expertise on a specific topic. They make regular posts about that topic on their preferred social media channels and generate large followings of enthusiastic, engaged people who pay close attention to their views." (https://influencermarketinghub.com/what-is-an-influencer/)

3   What measures are even appropriate to determine intelligence, given that most of our intelligence tests are heavily biased toward western, traditionally educated, white males, and then often only measure academic intelligence?

4   https://onlinelibrary.wiley.com/doi/abs/10.1111/j.1600-0447.2006.00895.x; https://www.sciencedirect.com/science/article/abs/pii/S1871519217300367; https://link.springer.com/article/10.1007/s00737-009-0059-4

5   https://www.psychologytoday.com/us/blog/born-love/201005/shocker-empathy-dropped-40-in-college-students-2000; https://www.psychologytoday.com/us/blog/the-narcissism-epidemic/201308/how-dare-you-say-narcissism-is-increasing; https://www.abc.net.au/radionational/programs/allinthemind/young-people-today-are-more-narcissistic-than-ever/5457236; https://bigthink.com/mind-brain/repeating-lies-people-believe-true-studies?rebelltitem=1#rebelltitem1

6   Wikipedia explains: "Colonialism is the policy of a polity seeking to extend or retain its authority over other people or territories, generally with the aim of developing or exploiting them to the benefit of the colonizing country and of helping the

colonies modernize in terms defined by the colonizers, especially in economics, religion, and health." (https://en.wikipedia.org/wiki/Colonialism)

7   See "The Hitchhiker's Guide to the Galaxy", by Douglas Adams

8   Plaster

9   https://www.hopkinsmedicine.org/health/wellness-and-prevention/the-brain-gut-connection; https://pubmed.ncbi.nlm.nih.gov/31728781/

10   https://www.verywellmind.com/the-self-medication-theory-of-addiction-21933

11   https://www.lifeline.org.au/about-lifeline/lifeline-information/statistics-on-suicide-in-australia; https://www.theguardian.com/australia-news/2018/sep/26/australias-rising-suicide-rate-sparks-calls-for-national-target-to-reduce-deaths; https://www.aihw.gov.au/reports/life-expectancy-death/deaths-in-australia/contents/leading-causes-of-death; http://www.abc.net.au/news/2016-11-30/system-for-suicide-prevention-rates-highest-10-years/8076780; https://healthtimes.com.au/hub/mental-health/37/news/aap/self-harm-and-suicidal-behaviour-among-australian-teenagers-rate-increased/2820/; https://ausprayernet.org.au/lifeline-calls-for-25-reduction-in-suicide-target/

12   https://www.frontiersin.org/articles/10.3389/fpsyt.2020.595696/full; http://www-personal.umich.edu/~daneis/symposium/2012/readings/Twenge2010.pdf; https://link.springer.com/article/10.1007/s11205-014-0647-1; https://www.medicalnewstoday.com/articles/322877#Why-does-U.S.-society-breed-anxiety?

13   https://www.provenmen.org/russell-brand-from-sex-addict-to-anti-porn-activist/

14   Brené Brown is an author and research professor at the University of Houston and She has spent the past two decades studying courage, vulnerability, shame, and empathy https://brenebrown.com/

15   Originally from Napoleon Hill, Think and Grow Rich

16   https://www.ncbi.nlm.nih.gov/pmc/articles/PMC1392256/; https://www.researchgate.net/post/What-is-the-scientific-position-on-the-inheritance-of-acquired-characteristics-Lamarckism

17   https://www.thegospelcoalition.org/article/why-you-should-consider-cancelling-your-short-term-mission-trips/

18   https://www.ncbi.nlm.nih.gov/pmc/articles/PMC2792572/; https://theconversation.com/loneliness-is-a-health-issue-and-needs-targeted-solutions-96262

19   https://inequality.org/facts/global-inequality/

20   https://guides.slv.vic.gov.au/whatitcost/groceries

21   See 1 Tim 2:13-14, although in a number of other scriptures such as Romans 5:12-21 make Adam responsible.

22   Eldredge, John. *Wild at Heart*. (Nashville, TN:Thomas Nelson Publications, 2001), 50-1

23   Joyner, Rick. *There Were Two Trees in the Garden*. (NC: Morningstar Publications, 2006.)

24   Dawkins, Richard. *The God Delusion*. (Boston, NY:Houghton Mifflin Co.)

25   https://www.psychologytoday.com/us/blog/psych-unseen/201607/the-narcissism-epidemic-and-what-we-can-do-about-it

26   https://www.nyu.edu/gsas/dept/philo/courses/materials/Narc.Pers.DSM.pdf

27   https://www.thetimes.co.uk/article/ending-religion-is-a-bad-idea-says-richard-dawkins-sqqdbmcpq

28   Orwell, George. *Animal Farm.* (London, UK: Secker and Warburg, 1945)

29   https://torahlifeministry.com/teachings/articles/23-bible-study/65-the-hebrew-v-greek-world-view.html

30   https://www.facebook.com/RussellBrand/videos/281655466731488/ and https://lisafeldmanbarrett.com/

31   https://www.skipmoen.com/2019/05/apostolic-by-lines-2/#comment-64218

About the author...

Ruth Embery lives with her husband, Martin, Daisy the Dog and two chickens ironically named Butter and Tandoori, in the beautiful Dandenong Ranges, just out of Melbourne, Australia. She is involved in a number of lay ministries, with a passion to see people healed, whole and living the life of abundant freedom that comes from real connection and relationship with Jesus Christ — Yeshua Messiah — promises. Ruth is available for speaking engagements and other ministry, including quiet days and can be contacted through ruth.embery@gmail.com, or you can find out more at www.ruthembery.com.

www.ingramcontent.com/pod-product-compliance
Lightning Source LLC
Chambersburg PA
CBHW050318010526
44107CB00055B/2297